YORK HANDB

GENERAL EDITOR:
Professor A.N. Jeffares
(*University of Stirling*)

STUDYING CHARLES DICKENS

K.J. Fielding

MA D PHIL (OXFORD)
Emeritus Professor of English Literature
University of Edinburgh

LONGMAN
YORK PRESS

Plate 6, the portrait of Ellen Ternan, is reproduced by courtesy of the Board of Trustees of the Victoria and Albert Museum.

YORK PRESS
Immeuble Esseily, Place Riad Solh, Beirut.

LONGMAN GROUP UK LIMITED
Longman House, Burnt Mill, Harlow,
Essex CM20 2JE, England
and Associated Companies throughout the World.

© Librairie du Liban 1986

First published 1986
Second impression 1990

ISBN 0-582-79283-5

Produced by Longman Group (FE) Ltd
Printed in Hong Kong

Contents

PLATES

Preface

This book is chiefly meant as an introduction to Dickens for students, and looks at his works partly in relation to his life and his life in relation to his times. There are many other good ways to approach Dickens, but this one has been chosen as a way of seeing clearly how he developed, what he wrote about, and what the expectations of his readers were. It is meant to be useful immediately after reading some of the novels. For further reading see the select bibliography. Though the present work has been rewritten it has a close relationship to my *Charles Dickens, A Critical Introduction* (1965), and I am gratefully indebted still further to many friends, institutions and other writers on Dickens.

Edinburgh, 1985   K.J. FIELDING

PLATE 1: Dickens in 1843: a drawing by R.J. Lane engraved by Edward Stodart.

Chapter 1

Early years: *Sketches by Boz*

CHARLES DICKENS WAS BORN on 7 February 1812, the second child and eldest son of John and Elizabeth Dickens. John was an improvident clerk in the Navy Pay Office, then stationed near Portsmouth, Elizabeth was from a slightly better class, her parents being respectable civil servants. Their son probably owed them a good deal, but confessed to no more than Mr Micawber as a sole inheritance from his father and Mrs Nickleby from his mother. His mother first taught her children at home, and was later ready to set up a school if she could have found any pupils, while John Dickens (the child of upper-class servants) shared her leanings to gentility, was affectionate and hard-working, but so easy-going with money that he was too ready to spend and borrow.

They moved to London, then (when Charles was five) to Chatham. Here he had a nurse named Mary Weller, learned comic songs, was told marvellous stories, and grew up 'a very queer small boy', with a habit of noticing everything about him. He was rather delicate, lively, good-tempered, cheerful and decidedly precocious.

At home the boy found a long series of novels in the attic, and crept up there to read – and to go on 'reading as if for life'. 'From that blessed room,' he wrote, 'Roderick Random, Peregrine Pickle, Humphrey Clinker, Tom Jones, the Vicar of Wakefield, Don Quixote, Gil Blas, and Robinson Crusoe, came out, a glorious host to keep me company. They kept alive my fancy . . . they, and the *Arabian Nights* and the *Tales of the Genii*'; and, one might add, the *Tatler*, the *Spectator*, Johnson's *Idler*, Goldsmith's *Citizen of the World*, and the works of Shakespeare. They stamped his imagination and sympathies in a way that was to leave a mark on everything he wrote.

The years in Chatham were Dickens's golden age. In later years, when in difficulties with a novel, he would put his characters into a coach and send them off to Chatham or to the adjoining Rochester. When he was a boy he once passed a great house at Gad's Hill with his father. 'When you are a man,' said his father, 'you might live there if you work hard enough.' When he was a man he bought it. Rochester and Chatham, and the countryside around, were a background against which he set some scene or other in almost every book he wrote.

Chatham was the birthplace of his fancy, though he hardly knew how to value it until he 'saw the falling cloud which was to hide its pictures from him for ever'.

The scene darkened when John Dickens was recalled to London: he was getting into debt. Charles's sister, Frances Elizabeth, went to the Royal Academy of Music and he himself wanted to go to school, but was kept at home to do odd jobs. He had no friends. He began writing little plays and essays, used to visit a godfather in Limehouse, and played with a toy theatre, while his greatest treat 'was to be out for a walk in the real town', to the Strand, or Covent Garden or the neighbouring and unsavoury Seven Dials. Yet all the time he felt neglected, for, as he afterwards said, he understood things then as well as he did later.

The blow fell when his father was arrested and taken off to the Marshalsea debtors' prison declaring, like Micawber, that the sun had set on him for ever. 'I really believed at the time,' Dickens said, 'that they had broken my heart.' In prison, John Dickens was visited by his family, and could still draw his salary untouched by his creditors. At home everything was pawned, Charles taking their things (including the books) to the pawnshop. Two days after his twelfth birthday his mother found him work in a blacking-factory.

There he was paid a few shillings a week, and worked in a dirty, rat-ridden warehouse, covering and labelling blacking-pots. Two other boys (one named Fagin) did the same. At first, young Dickens was kept apart from them, but afterwards they worked side by side. When his mother and the younger children joined their father in prison, he was found lodgings on his own. On Sundays, he would call for his sister, and they would join the others. For the rest of the week he looked after himself, with 'no advice, no counsel, no encouragement . . . no support, from any one'.

In later years Dickens was bitterly ashamed of this time, and spoke of it to no-one in his family but his wife. In fact it might never have been known if an acquaintance had not once mentioned that he had once met Dickens when he was a boy working at the warehouse. The remark was made to Dickens's friend and biographer, John Forster (1812-76); and, after Forster passed it on to him, Dickens was so moved that he wrote the whole story for him with much else about his childhood. Ultimately he decided to make use of the account in some of the earlier chapters of *David Copperfield*, in which he told how David was employed by a firm of wine-merchants, Murdstone & Grinby; and this part of the story of David's childhood bears a close resemblance to what happened to Dickens himself.

The difference between them is that David puts the blame on his ogre of a stepfather, and Dickens on his parents. He could never understand how they could see their son off to work in the blacking-factory, as happily as if they were sending him to Cambridge. He was a child of marked abilities, eager and quick and, strange as it may seem, already ambitious to grow up 'a learned and distinguished man'. Yet, he wrote, 'I know that, but for the mercy of God, I might easily have been, fòr any care that was taken of me, a little robber or a little vagabond.'

'I have no idea how long it lasted,' he wrote. (It may have been for a year.) John Dickens was left a fair-sized legacy and released, but did not think of releasing his son from the factory, until, at last, he had a slight quarrel with the factory manager, and took Charles away. Mrs Dickens wanted him to return, while his father 'said I should go back no more, and should go to school. I do not write resentfully or angrily,' said Dickens, 'but I never afterwards forgot, I never shall forget, I never can forget, that my mother was warm for my being sent back.'

Dickens never recovered from his experience, and to understand what lies at the heart of his feeling for children, the poor, debtors, and the unloved and outcast, you should read in Forster's pages all that is left of the strange document that Dickens once intended for his autobiography. As a result there developed in him a stern self-reliance, a liking for sympathy, and a burning desire to help others.

He was now sent to Wellington House Academy, a private school run 'by far the most ignorant man I have ever had the pleasure to know', 'whose business was to make as much out of us and to put as little into us as possible'. Fellow-pupils afterwards remembered Dickens as a smart lad, 'with a more than usual flow of spirits' and no special scholarly attainments. At home his father retired on a pension, taught himself shorthand and took up journalism; and, at fifteen, Dickens became a junior clerk in a solicitor's office. He 'didn't much like it', he said later. Even at the time he was ambitious, for he either persuaded his parents to support him, or used a small legacy to qualify himself as 'a first-rate parliamentary reporter'. In this he was influenced by his uncle, John Henry Barrow, formerly a reporter for *The Times*, who had just published a novel, deserted his wife, and founded a journal to record parliamentary debates as a rival to Hansard. Like Copperfield, Dickens learned a system of shorthand, 'about equal in difficulty to the mastery of six languages'. A friend said of him, 'there never *was* such a shorthand writer', and long afterwards Dickens half-seriously wrote, 'I daresay I am at this present . . . the best in the world!'

He began reporting in the ecclesiastical courts, then in the Law Courts – he might have heard cases there which were still continuing when he was writing about Jarndyce *v.* Jarndyce in *Bleak House*; and he was admitted to Parliament as a reporter about the age of nineteen.

Meanwhile he was preparing himself for a novelist's career in other
ways. His father was once asked, 'Pray, Mr Dickens, where was your
son educated?' 'Why, indeed, Sir – ha! ha! – he may be said to have
educated himself.' He studied hard to be an actor; as soon as he was
eighteen he began a course of reading at the British Museum; and he
learned all the ins and outs of London. 'I thought I knew something of
the town,' said a fellow-clerk, 'but after a little talk with Dickens, I
found that I knew nothing.'

He had time to fall in love with a girl named Maria Beadnell, but her
parents disapproved of the young reporter as a prospective son-in-law.
Dickens was desperate and, even twenty-five years later, annoyed
when Forster could hardly take it seriously:

> It excluded every other idea from my mind for four years . . . and . . .
> I went at it with a determination to overcome all the difficulties,
> which fairly lifted me up . . . and floated me away over a hundred
> men's heads. . . . Nothing can exaggerate that.

She was the Dora of *David Copperfield*. 'And just as I can never open
that book, as I open any other book,' he went on, he could not see her
again, after many years, 'without going wandering away over the ashes
of all that youth and hope in the wildest manner'. The romance fizzled
out, and Dickens forced himself to turn his back on it; but when they
were both middle-aged he told her that the effort had left him 'with a
habit of suppression which now belongs to me . . . which makes me
chary of showing my affection even to my children'.

As a reporter he worked for the radical *True Sun* in 1832, for his
uncle's *Mirror of Parliament* (1831-4), and from 1834 for the Whig
Morning Chronicle. Its editor was John Black (1793-1855), his 'first
hearty out-and-out appreciator', a man of marked independence of
mind and, according to the philosopher, John Stuart Mill (1806-73),
'the first journalist' to carry 'criticism and the spirit of reform into
English institutions'. These experiences must also have affected him.
His view of political life from the wings, a dislike of its impracticalities,
the agitation for reform and its dubious results, and the tedium of
politics all left their mark. We might add the effect of lively, more or
less radical and possibly better-educated companions, but this would
be mere guesswork as almost nothing is known of this part of his
career. We know rather more about his reporting of public meetings or
electioneering when Parliament was not sitting. He once spoke of
doing so under conditions 'of which . . . my modern successors can
form no adequate conception. I have often transcribed for the printer
. . . writing on the palm of my hand, by the light of a dark lantern, in a
post chaise and four, galloping through wild country'.

Already he had begun writing original pieces, and his first published work, a sketch called 'A Dinner at Poplar Walk', appeared in the old *Monthly Magazine* in December 1833. He contributed eight more unpaid sketches to the *Monthly*, including the first by 'Boz'. His talent for descriptive writing was recognised by his new employers and, when they launched the *Evening Chronicle* early in 1835, he was asked to write a series of twenty 'Sketches of London'. The editor was George Hogarth (1783-1870), a man of some cultivation, and a former friend of the novelist Sir Walter Scott (1771-1832). Dickens was invited to his home, where he met his eldest daughter Catherine, a pretty pink-and-white girl, with whom he soon fell in love – and she with him. The agonies of the Beadnell period were over: he took the dominant role, and insisted that she leave him time for his 'pursuits and labours' which were all undertaken for her future happiness. They were genuinely in love, but there was a new reserve about Dickens which shows through all the jokes and endearments in his letters.

By August 1835 he was ready to write further sketches for another magazine and to listen to the proposal that they should be collected. Dickens gladly accepted John Macrone's offer of £150 for their publication with illustrations by George Cruikshank (1792-1878). He wrote the extra ones needed for the book which was published in February 1836, the day after his twenty-fourth birthday.

The new *Sketches by Boz* was remarkable for its time and enthusiastically received. The sketch was an accepted form much commoner than is sometimes realised, but collected in a book his sketches made a fresh impact. They are unlike his reporter's work. Descriptive journalism hardly existed at the time, and when it did was swaddled in leader-writer's clichés; but, from description Dickens had advanced to comment and even to fiction, though here he was not seen at his best. Yet the new volumes earned him his first tribute of being 'inimitable' and unsurpassed in quickness of perception. Contemporaries saw that he was justified in hoping 'to present little pictures of life and manners as they really are' (Preface). The *Metropolitan Magazine* praised their 'startling fidelity'. 'Boz,' said another reviewer, 'is a kind of Boswell to Society.' The *Sketches*, in both series, was a work which could have stood alone, but which can be seen as leading directly to the world of *Oliver Twist*.

Chapter 2

Pickwick Papers and after

DICKENS MEANT TO BE MUCH MORE than a journalist, just as he had determined to be more than a reporter. He was proud to be an author, and in February 1836 had a further opportunity. He was approached by the recently established firm of Chapman & Hall, which was anxious to publish a humorous account of a sporting club to go with a series of illustrations by a well-known sporting artist, Robert Seymour (1800-36). They remembered Dickens's sketches in the *Chronicle*; and, as young men of ideas, made the surprising proposal that the work should come out in shilling numbers, 'then only known to me,' wrote Dickens, 'or I believe, to anybody else, by a dim recollection of certain interminable novels in that form, which used to be carried about the country by pedlars'.

Dickens saw his chance, and there was a brisk discussion about what sort of work it was to be. He insisted that, while glad to be illustrated by Seymour, he would not think of just providing a text to accompany the sketches. Nor was he willing to keep to the adventures of some comic sportsmen, wanting 'his own way with a freer range of English scenes and people'; but he would be happy to be published in monthly numbers of twenty-four pages – later thirty-two. There was no written contract. They shook hands on the agreement; and, as Dickens said, 'I thought of Mr. Pickwick, and wrote the first number'.

Yet, for the time being, it was easier said than done. Dickens was offered fourteen pounds a month, and wrote to Catherine to say, 'The work will be no joke, but the emolument is too tempting to resist'. His letters to her report progress, for now that their marriage was near both were interested in his success. He wrote about a fortnight later: 'I have at this moment got Pickwick, and his friends, on the Rochester coach, and they are going on swimmingly, in company with a very different character from any I have yet described [Alfred Jingle], who I flatter myself will make a decided hit.' He spent his days in reporting and nights in writing, and had to tell her, 'Pickwick must be attended to,' and again, 'the sheets are a weary length'. Yet by 15 March he finished two numbers in time for the first to be published at the end of the month, and on 2 April they were married. Years later, his brother-in-law wrote, 'As for the wedding, even Boswell could have had nothing to say, unless he had invented it'. Catherine was described as 'a bright, pleasant bride', and everyone was happy. Giving up the idea of following the Pickwickians to Rochester, they honeymooned at a cottage near Gravesend.

Pickwick, meanwhile was in difficulties. It sold only about four hundred copies, and the *Monthly Magazine* called it 'a signal failure'. To crown everything, Seymour retired to the summer-house at the bottom of his garden and shot himself. Fortunately Chapman & Hall decided to continue, and so Dickens interviewed would-be illustrators, turning down John Leech (1817-64), the humorous artist, and William Makepeace Thackeray (1811-63), the future novelist. The publishers took on someone else, then switched their choice to Hablot K. Browne (1815-82), known as 'Phiz'. With the exception of *Oliver Twist*, illustrated by Cruikshank, Browne remained Dickens's chief illustrator until after *Little Dorrit*.

Success came with the fifth number. The credit is sometimes given to Sam Weller who, in fact, was introduced only after the work was already beginning to catch on. Jingle, the Fat Boy, Wardle, the ball at Bath, the military review, Dingley Dell and the cricket-match with the Muggletonians – not to mention the Pickwickians themselves – all contributed to its popularity. *John Bull* thought it 'irresistibly good', and the *Metropolitan* said, '"Boz" marches on triumphantly, and has completely taken possession of our ear, and the hearts, too, of his countrymen'.

With No. 10 Dickens issued an 'Address' to say that he would keep to his original plan of giving only another ten because if prolonged the novel might suffer as 'a complete work'. He later followed the same scheme of twenty numbers for all his longer works. By this time sales had shot up to 40,000. As the novel was drawing to a close even the Tory *Quarterly* praised it handsomely: 'In less than six months' from its appearance,' it said, 'the whole reading public was talking about it . . . a new and decidedly original genius has sprung up.' 'Judges on the bench and boys in the street,' said Forster, 'gravity and folly, the young and old, those who were entering life and those who were quitting it' were all reading *Pickwick*.

'Phiz' sketched its hero, crowned king, on a throne resting on the works of the novelists Henry Fielding (1707-54), Tobias Smollett (1721-71) and Laurence Sterne (1713-68). The novelist Mary Russell Mitford (1787-1855) wrote to the poet Elizabeth Barrett (1806-61) that Dickens was 'the next great benefactor of the age' to Scott, and Dickens himself wrote to Chapman & Hall: 'If I were to live a hundred years, and write three novels in each, I should never be so proud of any of them, as I am of Pickwick, feeling as I do, that it has made its own way, and hoping . . . that long after my hand is withered as the pens it held, Pickwick will be found on many a dusty shelf.' His work was recognised as literature and its author as one of the greatest English novelists.

There has been some academic discussion about whether it is to be regarded as a novel; even Forster called it 'a series of sketches', and others have seen it as a kind of entertainment. It is certainly a novel of a kind. Yet the real merits of the book have little to do with any such dispute. Its bright comedy, its good humour and its raciness of style are apart from its form, though these qualities have sometimes been undervalued because *Pickwick* has been put in a class of its own. Edmund Wilson (1895-1972), the American critic, for instance, in his essay 'Dickens: The Two Scrooges', dismissed the humour as 'the aspect . . . that is best known' and spent most of his time on the lamentable interpolated stories. Yet *Pickwick* deserves attention both for its own sake and as Dickens's first novel.

Of course the work was largely improvised, but that improvisation was an art. The form of *Pickwick* was not carpentered but grew. It took shape like a genie from a bottle. It may be clumsy and disjointed, but it has movement and, once under way, a magnificent controlling persuasiveness and definite character. It has direction rather than form, a story rather than a plot, abundance, and a manner that gives a sense of completeness.

Dickens's 'form' is often to be found in his style and manner and, especially with *Pickwick*, in the comedy. Some of it lies in the ridicule of all he disliked and feared – cruelty, pomposity, self-deception, dishonesty, sanctimonious hypocrisy, and the use of forms, institutions and all kinds of restraints to suppress whatever seems free and natural. He exults in anyone's power to rise above his circumstances, whether through the extraordinary innocence and gullibility of a Pickwick or through the sharpness of a Sam Weller. The dramatic instinct of his comic characters, it has been said, is 'a sort of comic existentialism'. He had the ability, himself, to see things in a new light, and constantly used contrast.

At the start of the novel, Pickwick sets out on his travels through England, with a portmanteau, a notebook – and a telescope: the notebook being for his observations, and the telescope indicating jokingly that he wants to look at life from a distance without being involved. The novel runs on, precisely because he cannot help being involved: caught breaking into a girls' school, in a single lady's bedroom, in fights, duels, in court, in prison. What begins as simple humour develops an edge as, with the help of Sam Weller, Pickwick's eyes are slowly opened to the realities around him. It is a pattern of phrase, scene and plot. No doubt it is episodic, but, ranging from scene to scene throughout England, it gains an epic breadth, and its climax comes with Pickwick's trial for breach of promise and his committal to the Fleet prison.

Success was now assured for Dickens. He was accepted into literary society, and began making the kind of friends and acquaintances he was to keep afterwards, the MP, lawyer and dramatist Serjeant Thomas Noon Talfourd (1795-1854), the actor William Charles Macready (1793-1873), the comedian John Pritt Harley (1786-1858), the novelist William Harrison Ainsworth (1805-82), the artist Daniel Maclise (1806-70), and Leigh Hunt (1784-1859), the man of letters. He was soon taken up by the smart set at Holland House, where he met the novelist Sir Edward Bulwer Lytton later Lord Lytton (1803-73), the writer and wit, the Rev. Sydney Smith (1771-1845), the poet Walter Savage Landor (1775-1864), the dandy Alfred, Count D'Orsay (1801-52), the banker and poet Samuel Rogers (1763-1855), and the historian and social critic Thomas Carlyle (1795-1881). Carlyle found him 'A fine little fellow . . . clear blue, intelligent eyes . . . large, protrusive, rather loose mouth, a face of the most extreme *mobility*, which he shuttles about. . . . A quiet, shrewd-looking little fellow, who seems to guess pretty well what he is and what others are'.

Home life was quietly happy. Catherine's sister Mary wrote to a Scottish relative after she had stayed with the Dickenses: 'I think they are more devoted than ever . . . if that be possible – I am sure you would be delighted with him if you knew him he is such a nice creature and so clever. He is courted and made up to by all the literary Gentlemen.' A son, Charles Culliford Boz Dickens, was born on 6 January 1837, a daughter Mary on 6 March 1838, and a second daughter 'Katey' in October 1839. Eventually there were ten children in fifteen years. In 1837 they had moved to a moderate-sized house, 48 Doughty Street, where they stayed till December 1839, moving on then to a larger establishment, 1 Devonshire Terrace, Regent's Park.

Dickens's scope as a writer was now broadening out before him, presenting opportunities and problems. He had started his career, as he realised later, 'without influence, without money, without companions, introducer or adviser'; and although all these were to come he began by making mistakes.

He was doing too much, and still working for the *Morning Chronicle* till November 1836; meanwhile he had written a scorching pamphlet on the Sunday observance question, *Sunday Under Three Heads*; he had agreed to write a children's book by Christmas, though it never appeared; and he had two productions put on at the St James's Theatre, *The Strange Gentleman* and *The Village Coquettes*. For two hundred pounds he had agreed, in May, to finish a three-volume novel for Macrone, to be ready by the end of the year; and he wrote and collected another volume of *Sketches by Boz*, published in December.

No wonder that he burst out to Cruikshank, 'I cannot do more than one pair of hands and a solitary head can execute, and really am so hard pressed by now that I must have breathing time'.

Early in August, having, as he thought, persuaded Macrone to release him from his agreement, he undertook to write one more volume for the more powerful publisher Richard Bentley (1794-1871), and promised him the next after that. Then he had agreed to be editor of a magazine that Bentley was to bring out in the new year. For this he was to have forty pounds a month, in return for writing sixteen pages for each number. *Bentley's Miscellany*, as the new periodical was called, began in January 1837, and in February included the first instalment of Dickens's new serial, *Oliver Twist*. He remained in charge for just over two years, contributing powerfully to the magazine's success, though his career as editor was subject to a series of disagreements with Bentley.

The details of Dickens's disputes with publishers hardly concern us. What matters is why the disputes were so fierce, and what Dickens's reasons were. His relations with Chapman & Hall had been perfectly amicable. As we have seen, there was no written contract for *Pickwick* – an indication of the haphazard way in which authors and publishers conducted their business. In fact, a profit of between £14,000 and £20,000 is said to have been made from *Pickwick* in the first two or three years, out of which the publishers were sensible enough to allow Dickens £2,500.

It was unfortunate that Dickens had foolishly contracted to write several works for Bentley for not much more than a clerk's wages; and Bentley was anxious to hold him to his agreements. Dickens, on the other other hand, decided that he must negotiate his way to independence, buy back his contracts and, if need be, break them. Had Bentley been more generous or far-sighted he might easily have kept Dickens; but he had made his way by getting and holding the whip-hand over his authors on the assumption that if he had a legal contract, he could make them write him a best-seller. It was a bitterly competitive world. Novelists usually sold their works outright; there was no royalty system; they had no protection from international piracy, no rights over the dramatisation of their work, and had formed no association for self-protection. In calling Bentley 'a hound', 'a Brigand', and a 'dog', as he did in his letters, Dickens was only slightly heightening the normal idiom then current among writers.

The poet and journalist Thomas Hood (1799-1845), for example, resented the way in which publishers treated literature as a commodity. Thackeray sneered at them for not being 'gentlemen'. Dickens was exceptional only in seeing that authors were largely to blame for their own misfortunes, and in fighting back. He bought back *Sketches by*

Boz for over two thousand pounds and, after placing negotiations in the hands of his lawyers, eventually struggled free. As he later admitted to his solicitor:

> The Oliver agreement was my own making, and so was Pickwick. It was a consequence of the astonishing rapidity of my success . . . that the enormous profits of these books should flow into other hands than mine. It has always been so (and I speak from the knowledge of the lives of eminent and successful writers) and I cannot reasonably hope to be exempt from the curse which has fallen on all Professors of Literature.

He went on to say that, though he knew he could obtain a substantial advance from another firm of publishers, he would not touch it on principle: 'I do not take it, and will not; simply because I wish to free myself by my own exertions, and not by the assistance of "The Trade".'

In extricating himself from these difficulties, he owed much to the friendship he had formed with the forceful critic, John Forster. At this time Forster was about the same age as Dickens but already the influential literary and dramatic editor of the weekly *Examiner*. Coming from the north, bluffly energetic, he sometimes seemed 'a most unmanageable wild man' to his London friends. Yet he was prized as an adviser by men whose sensibilities he sometimes jarred on. The poets Alfred Tennyson (1809-92), Robert Browning (1812-89), Leigh Hunt and Walter Savage Landor all owed a great deal to him. Bulwer Lytton wrote, 'there is no safer adviser . . . no more refined critic'. Above all, he was useful to such friends because his wary shrewdness and aggressive pertinacity made him the ideal representative in negotiations with publishers.

Forster met Dickens on Christmas Day 1836. They renewed their acquaintance in April, and became fast friends. From about the fifteenth number of *Pickwick* there was nothing Dickens published that Forster did not first see and advise on. Their partnership did not escape the kind of embarrassing outbursts that troubled all Forster's literary friendships, but it lasted over twenty years, however strained and weakened in Dickens's last decade. In January 1839 Dickens wrote to him: 'Believe me . . . I see the value of you and appreciate the sterling openness and honesty of your heart, more and more . . . as I behold it in contrast with the hearts of other men' – a passage Forster left out of his biography of Dickens.

Chapter 3

Oliver Twist

THE WAY IN WHICH *Oliver Twist* came into being was almost as strange as *Pickwick*'s. As with *Pickwick* there were even doubts about how far Dickens saw it as a novel when he began. It has a topically journalistic air and form, which may come from its appearance in *Bentley's Miscellany* or go back to the sketches. Yet Dickens also gives the impression that he aimed at something much more. It was written over a long period for so short a work (December 1836 to September 1838), when he was almost submerged by other work and editorial duties that threatened to drive him back each month 'into a sea of manuscripts'. Yet he enjoyed writing it. Even on holiday he felt 'great difficulty in keeping my hands off Fagin and the rest of them in the evenings'; and, as the story came to a close, he fell on it 'tooth and nail'.

Towards the end he worked faster than he ever tried to do afterwards, and found it came easily. In later years he was particular about being undisturbed while writing; but when working on *Oliver*, his brother-in-law says that he once came into the sitting-room, and joined in the conversation, 'the feather of his pen still moving rapidly from side to side. . . . It was interesting to watch . . . the mind and muscles working (or, if you please, *playing*) in company, as new thoughts were being dropped upon the paper. And to note the working brow, the set of mouth, with the tongue tightly pressed against the closed lips, as was his habit'.

Clearly the novel had a serious purpose. After the hilarity of *Pickwick*, Forster explains, Dickens felt a change necessary 'for his own satisfaction'. He had the need for something new, more serious, and even leading to some practical result. He was delighted when his friend mentioned this in a review. But Forster hints at something more. He seems to say, if rather cryptically, that the interest roused by Fagin and his gang is due to human sympathies that everyone shares, and that some of the surprise and alarm they caused on their first appearance was because readers saw in them men and women like themselves. More precisely, he adds that the novel showed that 'being above' the need for 'depending on other people's opinions, and . . . being below it, are pretty much the same', and that 'it would startle both high and low to be conscious' of all 'that is implied in this close approximation'. He then nervously shies away from the subject, saying that he had better leave Fagin 'in his school of practical ethics', undisturbed. Yet this is exactly and precisely the point where actual criticism should begin.

Almost everyone who has written about *Oliver Twist* sees that its most interesting parts are those about the underworld. It is not just that Fagin and Sikes are more exciting than Dr Losberne and Mr Brownlow, but that they are shown more intelligently. More than this, Fagin and his gang are treated with greater sympathy. This is particularly true of Nancy: Dickens wrote, 'I hope to do great things . . . if I can only work out the idea I have formed of her'. The point about her is that she has never had a chance, and that though she might have been different it is too late for her to change. Almost the same point is made about the Artful Dodger and Charley Bates, which so moved Dickens's friend Serjeant Talfourd that, as the last chapters were written, he 'pleaded as earnestly' on their behalf 'in mitigation of judgement as ever at the bar' for any of his clients. In a sense, as the poet Algernon Charles Swinburne (1837-1909) says, even Fagin and Sikes were 'victims of circumstances'.

How far this is openly brought out is questionable but Forster shows that Dickens and his friends were well aware of it. In fact the whole tendency of the 'Newgate novels' of this time (to which *Oliver Twist* belongs) was to link fictional crime with radical views about society. The Law is meant to be utterly contemptible. Blathers and Duff, the Bow Street runners, are fools; we know from Bumble that 'the law is a ass'; and the sketch of Fang, the police-magistrate, shows it in all its brutal stupidity. That Fang was drawn from a real magistrate, Mr Laing, is irrelevant. He is introduced not because Dickens wanted to expose an individual, but because (as he said) the story required a harsh and insolent magistrate, and he preferred to sketch from life. It is fairly argued that when the Artful Dodger has his last fling, on committal for trial, Dickens is not just making fun of the Law but attacking its very rough justice. From the opening in the workhouse every institution is shown as contemptible, chiefly because they are all used to keep the lower classes from bothering those above them.

This was not new. From the time of *Paul Clifford* (1830) by Sir Edward Bulwer Lytton, in which the hero attacks the Law from the dock as the destructive instrument of the rich, some novelists had expressed their feelings of revolt. What is remarkable is that a man as passionate as Dickens should make his tale not only an outcry against society, but a powerful expression of a nightmare sense of evil, and of life's horror, disappointment, mystery and hope. For Dickens's main feat, the English critic John Bayley says, was in combining 'the genre of Gothic nightmare with that of social denunciation, so that each enhances the other'.

In doing so he had to overcome a central inconsistency. He meant to show that criminals were made not born. Yet Oliver, himself, brought

PLATE 2:   'Oliver asking for more', by George Cruikshank.

up in the workhouse, is naturally good. He is not even used as a bridge between the underworld and the comfortable surroundings of Chertsey. He is a pawn, sometimes on the black squares, sometimes on the white. But, as it happens, this matters less than might have been expected.

In a passage later dropped from his preface Dickens explained that 'in little Oliver' he 'wished to show . . . the principle of Good surviving through every adverse circumstance and triumphing at last'. Oliver is generalised, but Dickens knows how to turn this kind of convention to account. The absence of individuality only heightens the fact that the reader cares not just because it is Oliver, but, as Arnold Kettle (*b.* 1916) has said, 'every starved orphan in the world, and indeed everyone who is poor and oppressed and hungry is involved'.

The book shows a contrast between two worlds, which gives it some of its strange power. The criminal underworld seems dangerous. Fagin has fangs like a rat, and crawls forth at night like a 'loathsome reptile . . . in search of some rich offal for a meal'. By the end a whole mob rouses itself against Sikes with fury. Sikes and Fagin are menacing and corrupting, infesting and undermining society, which is right to feel insecure.

They are not merely representative of a criminal class, but of how evil mankind itself may become. The critic G. K. Chesterton (1874-1936) felt that Cruikshank's illustration of Fagin and Monks staring through an open window at Oliver asleep, gave him a sense that they were 'a kind of army of devils compassing earth and sky crying for Oliver's soul and besieging the house in which he is barred for safety'. They mean to corrupt him. The sensation that the book gives to the novelist Graham Greene (*b*. 1904) is one of despair: 'It has the eternal and alluring taint of the Manichee, with its simple and terrible explanation of our plight, how the world was made by Satan and not by God.'

We may read the book as a fantastic nightmare in which Oliver seeks for hope and purpose and his own identity, in scenes of loneliness, terror and betrayal. For Oliver is born into a world in which life is meaningless, death at hand, and pain and violence are common. This black confusion reaches out even when Oliver seems secure again with Mr Brownlow. Only chance defeats evil; and, even when the happiness of a loving family has been restored to Oliver, he learns that it is 'a world of disappointment', since 'poor Dick' (the childhood friend he had hoped to help) is 'dead!' And there is the horror of his visit to Newgate and 'the Jew's last night alive' to come.

The forces of good, moreover, are often tame; they confront wrongdoers only after desperate fictional contrivances and without evil's concentration of purpose. On the other hand it is a strained interpretation to read the novel as a work of despair rounded off with false optimism. It is fundamentally optimistic in arguing that crime is caused by circumstance. We know that even Fagin's corruption is caused by man and can be checked. When Oliver is first taken care of, 'it was a solemn thing to hear . . . the sick child recounting a weary catalogue of evils and calamities which hard men had brought upon him. Oh! if when we oppress and grind our fellow-creatures, we bestowed one thought upon the dark evidences of human error, . . . if we heard, but one instant in imagination, the deep testimony of dead men's voices, which no power can stifle . . . where would be the injury and injustice, the suffering, misery, cruelty and wrong, that each day's life brings with it!'

Goodness cannot be destroyed. Nancy's love for Sikes is right; Charley has the courage to attack him; Oliver impulsively leaps through the window to pursue Sikes and Fagin when they stare in at him, for he is 'a child of noble nature and a warm heart' in whom, as Rose Maylie says, 'the Power which has thought fit to try him . . . has planted . . . affections and feelings' that might honour his elders. And so, Dickens writes, 'men who look on nature, and their fellow-men, and cry that all is dark and gloomy, are in the right; but the sombre colours are reflections from their own jaundiced eyes and hearts. The real hues are delicate and need a clearer vision'. This is the teaching of Henry Fielding's novels expressed with Dickens's power, imaginatively concentrated with the intensity of fable. Its teaching is that only in love we can live purposefully and happily; and this holds together Oliver's progress, the tale of his mother's unhappy love, the stories of Harry and Rose and the comic downfall of Bumble, and makes a tragedy of Sikes's murder of Nancy. The betrayal and murder of Nancy in spite of her love destroys Sikes himself, and breaks up Fagin's band.

Because of its terrifying power the work had a mixed reception, though this has sometimes been forgotten. Bumble, Fagin and Sikes have somehow come to be accepted as typically English! The English critic Arnold Kettle even believed it a 'curious comment on Victorian civilization' that it was thought 'suitable reading for children'. Yet the early Victorians at least hardly thought it fit for adults. A contemporary critic says that 'the most striking thing . . . was that it disclosed . . . an unsuspected gradation of ranks in . . . the lower orders' (*Cornhill*, 10:411). Some readers refused to admit its truth, while to others – such as Sir Francis Burdett (1770-1844) – it was an eye-opener. At this time, after forty years in parliament, he wrote to his daughter (later Dickens's friend) Angela Burdett Coutts in shocked wonder: 'It is very interesting, very painful, very disgusting, & as the Old Woman at Edinburgh, on hearing a preacher on the sufferings of Jesus Christ said, Oh dear I hope it isn't true. Whether anything like it exists or no I mean to make enquiry for it is quite dreadful, and, to Society in this country, most disgraceful.'

Well might the *Quarterly* write that 'one half of mankind lives without knowing how the other half dies'. Yet others neither knew, nor wished to know. The writer John Gibson Lockhart (1794-1854) had found even *Pickwick* 'damned low'. Henry Fox (1791-1846), the diplomatist, thought *Oliver* 'painful and disgusting', and Lord Melbourne (1779-1848), the prime minister, disliked 'the low debasing style'; and, far from recommending it for children, the *Edinburgh Review* and the *Quarterly* expressed consternation at its possible effect on 'the rising generation'. Dickens, as the novelist and critic Mrs Margaret Oliphant (1828-97) said later, was clearly 'a *class* writer . . . one of the advocates of the plea of the Poor *versus* Rich' – and the rich were alarmed.

It is often reasonably said that some knowledge of the historical background is needed to appreciate the novel fully. But it is more an awareness of differences in taste and feeling that is needed, rather than an understanding of the sort of historical question usually raised, such as whether the workhouse scenes were meant to satirize the Old Poor Law or the New. The novel was never meant as an attack on particular institutions, but on the spirit behind them which remained largely unchanged. Over twenty-five years later Dickens refers in the postscript to *Our Mutual Friend* to reports on workhouse hospitals that had just appeared in the *Lancet* which showed how the same kind of men were in charge as in the days of Bumble. 'The truth is,' wrote the authors, 'that the unfortunate influence of the early traditions of the Poor Law Commissioners lingers with fatal tenacity'. The belief of the journalist and general writer Harriet Martineau (1802-76) that the evils of the system ended with the New Poor Law of 1834 hardly deserves consideration. Some people neither knew, nor wished to know.

It must be clear that though Dickens's novels were neither works of instruction nor propaganda, they were often closely concerned with public problems. It has been said, in Dickens's day and ours, that the social abuses he castigated had ceased to exist when he wrote about them. But do not let us pretend that *Pickwick* and *Bleak House* are not to some extent about the Chancery prisoner and law reform; that juvenile crime, prostitution and the Poor Law, as they affect humanity, are not part of the subject of *Oliver Twist*; that there was no basis for the satire in *Chuzzlewit*; that class is not one of the concerns in *Dombey*, and that *Our Mutual Friend* had no direct message for its first readers. The very opposite was a source of pride to Dickens and of strong offence to some of his public. Almost alone among novelists, he was able to bring his public figure, his private person, the narrator of his fiction and the 'Charles Dickens' of his journalism effectively into combination.

It is one of Dickens's greatest qualities that although he combined the two voices of novelist and public spokesman, he could face the terrible inhumanity of much of the mid-nineteenth century without being helplessly appalled or losing his strong concern for fellow-men. Many had come to terms by ignoring it, like Burdett and the earliest readers of *Oliver Twist*. A clear impression of the effect that the life of the time had on a sensibility unhardened and unprepared for it, can be found in the earlier part of the journal of the American writer Nathaniel Hawthorne (1804-64). Hawthorne first landed at Liverpool in 1854 and found that the poverty-stricken English street was 'a monstrosity unknown on our side of the Atlantic'. At first he was so fascinated by its squalor that he says, 'I often turned aside from the

PLATE 3:   Dickens, his wife and her sister Mary: a drawing by Daniel Maclise engraved by Stodart.

prosperous thoroughfares', and purposely went 'among precincts that reminded me of some of Dickens's grimiest pages'. As time went on his journal shows that he kept his compassion, but he could not see the people of the streets as anything but 'maggots in cheese . . . disgusting', like 'vivacious bugs and insects'; until finally he returned to the beaten path, gave up making a record, and turned his journal into an ordinary tourist's diary. It was a normal response.

  Yet Dickens did not write or feel about people like this. In contrast to Hawthorne and almost all men of his time, Dickens's extraordinary quality lies not only in his power of observing what was before him without recoiling, but in never losing the power of communicating his sense of humanity. When he died, a friend wrote that there had never been a writer of fiction who took such a real and living interest in the actual world about him. 'Its many sorrows, its terrible injustice, its calamities, went to his heart.' If we lose the sense of communicating with him either because of our concern with unimportant historical details or because we are exclusively concerned with some limited aspect of his technique, we miss something essential.

Meanwhile *Oliver* showed both Dickens and his public that he possessed new powers. He was still squandering them in various minor literary and dramatic activities; and, when he started *Oliver*, he was not above undertaking the memoirs of the famous clown Grimaldi; as it neared completion he complained to his publisher that the tasks he had set himself 'would have been beyond Scott himself'. There was now no other writer of similar stature for Dickens to compare himself to.

It was while he was writing *Oliver* that tragedy came into his own life. Since marriage, he and Catherine had often been visited by one of her younger sisters, Mary Hogarth. She was seventeen, naturally charming, sweet-natured, gay and beautiful, and he afterwards declared 'that so perfect a creature never breathed. . . . She had not a fault'. One evening, in May 1837, they came home from the theatre; Mary was taken ill and died. 'Of our sufferings,' wrote Dickens, 'I will say nothing. . . . Thank God she died in my arms, and the very last words she whispered were of me.' He slipped a ring from her finger which he wore until his own death; and, as long as he lived, she seems to have had first place in his memory.

He remembered her with love and affection, and a passionate intensity which almost overwhelmed him. He brought her character into his books, wanted to be buried by her side, and for months dreamed of her every night – until he told his wife and the dreams stopped.

Chapter 4

Nicholas Nickleby

THOUGH MARY'S DEATH made a break in his writing, Dickens left himself little time for grief. In July he and Catherine went on holiday in Belgium; then August and September were spent at Broadstairs at work on *Oliver*. Before a dinner to celebrate finishing *Pickwick* in November, he signed a more favourable contract with Chapman & Hall for another novel, to which he turned in the new year.

He thought carefully about its subject, knowing how hard it would be to live up to *Pickwick*, and he soon hit on the idea of writing about the Yorkshire schools, boy-farms where unwanted children were disposed of, a subject he felt sure he could make tell. He had heard of these places as a child when someone told him about a schoolmaster who had operated on a boy's suppurating abscess 'with an inky penknife'. At once he collected a letter recommending him as an anxious parent looking for a school, conscripted his illustrator Hablot Browne, and set off by coach through heavy snow to Barnard Castle.

They made a quick survey, taking special note of a school kept by one William Shaw where two boys had gone blind from neglect. The local solicitor advised them not to send a boy there while there was a horse to hold in London or a gutter to lie in. No more was needed. Dickens's quick eye had seen enough to give the tale local colour; Browne had a thumb-nail sketch of the one-eyed Shaw. They returned to London, and in a few weeks Wackford Squeers met Nicholas.

On sale in April, the work was an immediate success. It was so astoundingly varied! The grim realities of Dotheboys Hall were presented with an oddity and gusto that left his hearers breathless with horror and laughter. Squeers, said George Gissing (1857-1903), the English novelist and critic, was treated less as the study of a human being, than 'the representative . . . of a vile institution'. The narrative was vigorous and lively, rapidly leading to the moment when, unable to bear Squeers's brutality to the boys any more, Nicholas bursts out with 'I will not stand by and see it done', seizes his cane, and beats 'the ruffian till he roared for mercy'.

Nicholas's outcry is in exactly the same words as Nancy's when Fagin lifts his club against Oliver: it is Dickens's declaration that he means to protest at injustice and cruelty and that nothing will stop him. It was about this time, says G. H. Lewes (1817-78), a friendly critic who knew him, that his 'vivacity and sagacity' had become 'weighted with a seriousness which . . . became . . . prominent in his conversation and writings. He had already learned to look upon the world as a scene where it was "everyone's duty" to make the lot of the miserable Many a little less miserable. . . . He was sometimes laughed at for the importance he seemed to attach to everything relating to himself . . . but this belonged to his quality. *Il se prenait au sérieux*, and was admirable because he did so.'

A comic treatment of subjects of grim seriousness was now the staple of the Dickens novel. But it would be a mistake to underestimate the gaiety of *Nickleby*. The Mantalinis, the Kenwigses and the Crummleses are effortlessly funny. The oddity of Newman Noggs is pleasing. Fanny Squeers's letter to Ralph Nickleby is in Dickens's vein of fanciful humour: 'My pa requests me to write to you, the doctors considering it doubtful whether he will ever recuvver the use of his legs which prevents his holding a pen. We are in a state of mind beyond everything, and my pa is one mask of brooses both blue and green likewise two forms are steepled in his Goar. . . . He assaulted my ma with dreadful violence, dashed her to the earth, and drove her back comb several inches into her head. A very little more and it must have entered her skull.'

Brightest and best is Mrs Nickleby who burbles refreshing inanities, as fatuous and foolish as a well-meaning mother can be. She is said to have been drawn from Elizabeth Dickens who, true to character, never recognised herself to the last. 'Mrs Nickleby herself,' Dickens wrote, 'sitting bodily before me . . . once asked me whether I really believed there ever was such a woman!'

Two characters who are drawn from definite 'originals' are the Cheeryble brothers, based on what Dickens had heard of two Manchester businessmen, Daniel and William Grant. The elder alone is said to have given away more than six hundred thousand pounds in his lifetime. Perhaps too much was once made of these characters in critical discussions of the book. Walter Bagehot (1826-77) editor of the *Economist* as well as literary critic, thought that 'the Messrs Cheeryble were among the stupidest of Dickens's characters'. 'The harm they must have done, those two jolly old boys!' wrote Gissing. Yet the whole book is largely an extravaganza, not to be taken literally, and such figures as the Cheerybles stand for Dickens's faith in human goodness.

The question of 'originals' needs to be put in a different form. It might be taken as an expression of a simple and innocent pleasure in seeing the likeness and transformation. Yet it is also a chance to see Dickens at work, a light on the nature of fiction, and often an insight into a specific situation. It can be childishly reductive if we simply set about pairing off imaginary places and characters with actual counterparts.

Nor, if we are studying Dickens for the first time, may this be exactly the best place to start. But it was vital for Dickens. We have just seen how he could hardly begin *Nickleby* without first visiting Yorkshire, setting out in deep snow on a long coach-journey, just to catch a glimpse of the Squeers 'original' through a crack in the door; just as he could not envisage the setting for *Hard Times* without going to Preston, or create even Slackbridge without using what he had seen of a strike leader called Grimshaw. There were many reasons: his desire to communicate, to show a complex situation in a simple form, his acceptance that novelistic fiction was related to actuality, a delight in imitation, and the realisation that however fantastic his imagination might be (and indeed just *because* it was so inclined to fantasy) it needed actuality. To bring the two together was a fictional metaphor, necessary for Dickens whether clearly noticed by his readers or not. It is also part of a *pretence* which loses all purpose if we cannot sense what is happening.

So *Nicholas Nickleby* means more if we do not forget the grim reality of the contemporary scene; but, even to Bagehot, it had begun to seem to show 'the breadth of platitude'. Yet, platitudinous or not, a belief in health and sanity, decency and kindness, is at the core of the whole book. Since it is not developed systematically the pattern is simpler than in the later novels, but expresses fundamentally the same idea as *Little Dorrit* and *Great Expectations* – that those who shut themselves off from their fellows end unhappily and bring retribution on themselves.

Since *Nickleby* is essentially a young man's novel, this belief is developed through Love. It is *romantic* in the popular sense: love, true and false, concealed, devoted, disregarded and fulfilled is its chief theme. It opens by telling how Nicholas's two grandparents had married 'out of mere attachment', and that 'two people who cannot afford to play cards for money, sometimes sit down for love'. It ends with an orgy of weddings when Nicholas marries Madeline, Frank Cheeryble Nicholas's sister Kate, and Tim Linkinwater Miss La Creevy. 'How dare you think, Frank', cries the elder Cheeryble, 'that we would have you marry for money when youth, beauty and every amiable virtue . . . were to be had for love?' – 'All love', thinks Ralph, '– bah! that I should use the cant of boys and girls – is fleeting . . . originates in blindness and is fed by vanity.'

Love is also essentially ridiculous: Mrs Nickleby is enraptured by the lunatic next door, Madame Mantalini enslaved by her absurd husband, Fanny tries to trap Nicholas, and Mr Lillyvick insists on putting his head 'in the noose' with Miss Petowker. It may also be sinister: Kate is pursued by Lord Frederick Verisopht and Sir Mulberry Hawk; the old lord who hovers round the trying-on room at the gownshop has eyes for no-one else; Smike's hopeless love for her is a bitter one; and the repulsive old miser Gride has a nasty relish for Madeline, 'fresh, lovely, bewitching and not nineteen, . . . ripe and ruddy lips that to look at is to long to kiss, beautiful clustering hair that one's fingers itch to play with'.

Even more than in Dickens's other works, the main burden of *Nicholas Nickleby* is that there is a virtue in the frank expression of decent human feelings, and perversion when they are thwarted and suppressed. As Dickens meant Oliver Twist to be 'a principle of Good surviving through all adverse circumstances' (Preface), so he meant Kate to stand for tender and attractive purity. Even her uncle sometimes softens towards her. Lord Frederick dies as a result of a quarrel in which he has taken her part. We see that Squeers's school is successful mainly because it is a place where natural children and stepsons can be sent and forgotten, that Ralph's marriage was a secret one and made for money, that he curses his offspring, and that he ends by hanging himself 'immediately below the trapdoor . . . in the very place to which the eyes of his own son', whom he had helped to hound to death, had often been turned 'in childish horror . . . years before'.

It is not a 'well-written' novel, and many of its tricks are transparent. Some of the scenes with the Vincent Crummles company, for example, help us to understand Dickens's methods and our delight in them. Already in *Oliver Twist* he had compared the sudden transitions of the story to those of 'all good murderous melodramas' – which are absurd only if we stand apart from them. So one frequent solution was to stand apart, to be absurd, and thus arouse the reader's sense of reality. In *Nickleby*, for example, there is nothing so stagey as the serious part of the story, and nothing so comic as the scenes in which we are asked to hold aloof just because they are obviously a pretence – those with the Crummles players. Yet when Crummles at last says good-bye to Nicholas, he is seen as a man of sincerity and feeling, as 'not a jot of his theatrical manner' remains and he puts out his hand 'with an air which, if he could have summoned it at will, would have made him the best actor of the day in homely parts'. Almost all Dickens's best comedy lies in pretence, and all Dickens's characters involuntarily act out their parts.

He delighted in shams because he saw through them so sharply. They seemed almost necessary to him. In a similar way, in the theatre of his time the element of escapism was so much stronger because men needed to escape urban industrialism and utilitarian philosophy. It is true that Dickens could conscientiously praise the serious drama because it was 'founded on an eternal principle of human nature . . . an inborn delight and interest in a living representation of the actions, passions, joys and sorrows of mankind'. More usually, as he used to

speeches, he felt that it was 'cheering', and that it 'afforded
. am very fond of the play,' he once told his hearers, and 'I dare
‹ feeling peculiar to a theatre is as well known to everybody here
.‹ is to me, of having for an hour or two quite forgotten the real
‹orld, and of coming out into the street with a kind of wonder that it
should be so wet, and dark, and cold.' He praised it as a 'fleeting
fairyland'; and such, without his comic sense, would have been the
tendency of much of his earlier fiction. Comedy often gives him the
chance to be serious; for without comic overtones he would never have
allowed himself to write of Fagin's den or Dotheboys Hall; they
offered scope to his gifts which he might otherwise have wasted in 'fine'
writing. His view of life is essentially comic in these earlier novels
because he sees life as full of necessary but enjoyable pretences: a
fiction that is needed because however much we decry human
absurdity it is better than the actuality in which men live; for, so he
says, 'it will generally be found that those who sneer habitually at
human nature . . . are among its worst and least pleasant examples'. He
even relishes comedy and pretence for their own sake: Squeers's oddly
enjoyable indifference to human suffering, Bumble's pomposity,
Mantalini's gentility, all come from the same mould as the self-
deceptions of the Pickwickians and the fascinating deceits of Quilp,
Pecksniff and Micawber. Comic pretence is Dickens's 'fancy' in
another form, the harsh suppression of which he believed fatal to the
human spirit.

Considered seriously, the world of the earlier novels is often chaotic
and heartless. When Nicholas and Smike reach London at last, they
pass into 'streams of people, apparently without end . . . hurrying
forward . . . while vehicles of all shapes and makes, mingled up
together in one moving mass like running water'. And, as they dash on,
they see a strange procession of objects, all man needs for luxury – and
for death:

> guns, swords, pistols, and patent engines of destruction; screws and
> irons for the crooked . . . drugs for the sick, coffins for the dead,
> churchyards for the buried – all these jumbled each with the other
> . . . seemed to flit by in motley dance like the fantastic groups of the
> old Dutch painter [Holbein], and with the same stern moral for the
> unheeding, restless crowd.

Squeers's centre of operations, at the Saracen's Head near Newgate, is
said to be 'at the very core of London'; typical of the city to Dickens, 'a
whirl of noise and motion' from the midst of which men 'have been
hurried violently and swiftly from the world, when the scene has been
rendered frightful with excess of human life'; a world of tragedy and
comedy; a life in which nothing may seem of importance but the

individual, yet in which it is all the more necessary for people to meet in love and friendship through charity and laughter.

To understand the Dickens of these earlier works we must include the interpretation given by the American critic Hillis Miller in his *Charles Dickens, The World of His Novels*:

> From the point of view of the characters themselves, this kind of life may be defined in a single word, isolation. Each of these novels . . . has at its centre characters who are alienated from society, and the situation of all is to be surrounded by an inimical world, a world which refuses to support or recognize their existence. . . . The happy endings of these novels do not . . . represent an adequate analysis of the complexities of the theme of direct and intimate relations between man and man in society.

This is true of the endings, and what is said of the characters can be abundantly illustrated. Nicholas Nickleby himself can become weary and despondent, not only at his misfortunes but at life itself, for:

> now, when he thought how regularly things went on, from day to day in the same unvarying round; . . . how few there were who tenanted the stately houses, and how many of those who lay in noisesome pens, or rose each day and laid them down each night, and lived and died, father and son, mother and child, race upon race, generation upon generation, without a home to shelter them or the energies of one single man directed to their aid; how . . . in seeking . . . the bare means of a most wretched and inadequate subsistence, there were women and children in that one town, divided into classes . . . and reared from infancy to drive most criminal and dreadful trades; how ignorance was punished and never taught; how jail doors gaped and gallows loomed . . . how much injustice, misery, and wrong there was, and yet how the world rolled on from year to year, alike careless and indifferent; . . . when he thought of all this, and selected from the mass the one slight case on which his thoughts were bent, he felt, indeed, there was little ground for hope, and little reason why it should not form an atom in the huge aggregate of distress and sorrow.

True as it may be that the happy endings are not enough, there is no doubt that the spirit of the whole novel checks any tendency to despair. It is not just the comic spirit, for it cannot be that misfortune is laughable: rather that, in *Nickleby* (Chapter 53) as in *Oliver*, 'the darkest side of the picture' can be shifted 'at will'; nor does this follow simply because Dickens says so, for the darkness is counterbalanced not just by sentiment but by a strong and outright moral protest and urgent demand for reform.

pt 'the darkest side' would lead to despair; but men *can* be children taught, wrongs redressed. Compare Nicholas's ge through the streets with his uncle's return home after he has int that he has destroyed his own son, Smike. Ralph passes by a mean burial ground . . . a rank unwholesome spot' where lie the 'grisly family', the 'dear departed brothers and sisters of the ruddy clergyman who did his task so speedily when they were hidden in the ground'; he sees another miming of the Dance of Death, gives a vacant laugh, and turns home to take his life. But Nicholas's decision was 'to act'. Dickens's reformism is not just a social comment on his own times, but part of his fictional philosophy and way of life.

Nickleby took a full eighteen months to write, overlapping with *Oliver Twist* and *Barnaby Rudge*. When Dickens went to insure his life, about this time, doctors told him he was working too hard, and he admitted that 'if this were to go on much longer, I should "bust" the boiler'. The book was finished in September 1839, when he wrote 'the discovery is made, Ralph is dead, the loves have come all right and I have now only to break up Dotheboys and the book together'. He was in tremendously high spirits.

The last thing was to dedicate the book to the Shakespearian actor, William Macready, and make arrangements for a Nicklebeian dinner. Macready, whose friendship had grown closer all the previous year, was touched and confided to his diary that it was 'as great' an honour 'as a man can receive'. In proposing Dickens's health, he 'spoke of him as one who made the amelioration of his fellow-men the object of all his labours'. 'I did not get through it well,' he added. A week later he was godfather at the christening of Dickens's third child, Catherine Macready (Katey).

Chapter 5

The Old Curiosity Shop and *Barnaby Rudge*

WHILE FINISHING *Nickleby* Dickens was thinking of what to do next. He wanted to be more independent of his publishers and free from the grinding need to write. His idea was to start a weekly periodical, not all of which he would write himself, which would be a cross between contemporary magazines and the *Spectator* of Joseph Addison (1672-1719) or *The Bee* of Oliver Goldsmith (1728-74). It might start 'with some pleasant fiction relative to the origin of the publication,' and introduce 'a little club' the members of which would 'tell their personal histories'. It need have no continuous story, but just offer an entertaining series of articles on all kinds of subjects from Old London to topical satire. Once well established, the editor might even travel, in Ireland or America, and write home what came to mind.

The proposal was not as strange as it sounds. Such magazines were already springing up, and only ten years later Dickens was to show what could be done with *Household Words*. A genuinely new periodical might have been successful: Dickens's proposal was wrong in being imitative and sentimentally backward-looking. He had a clearer idea about the financial arrangements, made with Chapman & Hall, but went on with his scheme about a curious old man, living alone, with an affection 'for an old quaint queer-cased clock' in which he kept a collection of miscellaneous 'manuscripts in the old, deep, dark, silent closet'. These were to be read and discussed by the club. Altogether it was a hopeless proposition and, after the first number had been sold in enormous numbers, sales suddenly flopped.

Dickens was forced to evolve a continuous serial tale to suit old Humphrey instead of a miscellany. Happily he had the idea of the story of Little Nell and, though he began hesitantly, he was soon able to create enough characters to carry it on. Yet he found writing in weekly numbers another problem, and felt that the form left him with hardly 'room to turn'. All through the summer he kept writing *Master Humphrey's Clock*: 'Wind, wind, wind, always winding am I; and day and night the alarum is ringing in my ears, warning me it must not run down.' He kept on through two seaside holidays at Broadstairs until, at Christmas, he was far enough ahead to think of the ending. Forster says, 'I never knew him wind up any tale with such sorrowful as this.' 'All night,' Dickens told him, 'I have been pursued ﹍ild; and this morning I am unrefreshed and miserable.' From ﹍st he had identified her with Mary Hogarth, and the whole trend ﹍ne story had been towards her death. To the author and art critic ﹍ohn Ruskin (1819-1900), she was 'butchered for the market', and Dickens blushed when his friend Macready said that 'he was cruel'; but he was sincere in his despair at what he had to write. 'Old wounds bleed afresh when I only think of doing it,' he wrote, 'dear Mary died yesterday when I think of this story.'

In discussing Nell one can only go on to the defensive, and it is not enough to argue that she was enormously popular at the time. True, Lord Jeffrey (1773-1850), the old judge and critic of the *Edinburgh Review*, declared that there was 'nothing so good as Nell since Cordelia'. But, without trying to condemn the whole age, there is something peculiar about Dickens's well-known contemporaries who enlisted as her admirers – the historian Thomas Babington Macaulay (1800-59), Washington Irving (1783-1859), the Rev. Sydney Smith, Walter Savage Landor, the Danish story-teller Hans Andersen (1805-75), John Forster and the poet and translator Edward FitzGerald (1809-83). There seems a strain of self-pity about their liking. It has been said that we ought not to suppose that in different periods readers can be – as it were – on different wavelengths. But what the tale and its reception suggest is that it belongs to a different kind of literature from the *novel*. On the one hand it is an allegory, on the other it shows the peculiarly romantic elements of the literary folk tale. Readers of folk tales, of such works as Andersen's 'The Story of a Mother', or *The Story Without an End* by the German Friedrich Wilhelm Carové (1789-1852), or the tales of the brothers Jacob (1785-1863) and Wilhelm (1786-1859) Grimm or of 'Novalis' (the pseudonym of George Friedrich von Hardenberg, 1772-1801) will perceive the parallels. The reader of Dickens has to be alert to respond to many different kinds of literature as he reads.

He tried to make this clear. Once he had finished he returned to touch up the opening chapter and explained that 'the lonely figure of the child' was one 'who seemed to exist in a kind of allegory'. He allows Humphrey to explain that she is a dream child, 'holding her solitary way among a crowd of wild grotesque companions; the only pure, fresh, youthful object in the throng'. He feels carried away by the idea 'at a great pace', but 'resolves to go to bed and court forgetfulness'. But, from that point, the tale continues as if it had the atmosphere of a dream. The illustrations of Nell foster this, as does the accompanying account of how her friends at last look down on her 'on her little bed' and see her sweet but unchanged face as having 'passed like a dream through the haunts of misery and care'.

It is strange how the story developed consistently though at first unplanned. It goes back to the greatest of all tales in the dream convention, by the author who 'dreamed a dream' and saw a man clothed in rags, with 'a book in his hand, and a great burthen upon his back'. As they set out on their journey Nell and her grandfather are described as 'two pilgrims'; and when they have their first rest and look back towards London where the cross of St Paul's glitters above the smoke, Nell thinks of the *Pilgrim's Progress* (1678), and says, 'I feel as if we were both Christian, and laid down on this grass all the cares and trouble we brought with us; never to take them up again.'

The whole course of their journey is emblematic of the changing scenes of life: the graveyard where they meet Punch and Judy, the race-course, the green lanes, the waxworks, the wild journey through the Black Country, and the last procession up the snow-covered path to the churchyard. Yet the trouble is that the tale is never more than *like* an allegory; and that whereas in a genuine allegory the story and its meaning should each have an independent vitality, the tale of the girl and her grandfather has not enough living belief behind it. With all the references to heaven and the angels, Dickens himself was not convinced; for, in all his sorrow for Mary Hogarth, he told Forster, 'I can't preach to myself the schoolmaster's consolation, though I try'. He was clever enough to make it mean something to others, but only to those who were willing to believe. It was a bold attempt, and successful for the time being. But, in the long run, many of the passages describing Little Nell have only a tarnished prettiness.

It has to be read as a kind of fairy-tale; and it is making heavy weather to see it in terms of archetypes, primordial symbols, and myths of the ancient world. Fairy-tales belong to the same world, but as seen by a child. The stock of characters in the novel consists of children, dwarfs, midgets, Punch-and-Judy-men and waxwork women; the book's pictures of life, of the churchyard, the factory, the town or country are often a child's. The appeal of Nell's innocence is to age, it is linked with the old grandfather, the schoolmaster, and elder brother; but elsewhere the tale's wonders and delights belong to a world of goblins, ogres and giants. Nell's bed in the first chapter (added after serialisation) is one 'a fairy might have slept in'; we are led to the final chapter by 'the magic reel'. Quilp lives in an 'ogre's castle', 'the Marchioness is a Genie', and the Garlands' fairy cottage reminds Kit of giants' castles, princesses and dragons.

The story is saved from insipidity by sharp observation, satire and comic dramatisation. In the scene when Nell is turned away by the schoolmistress Miss Monflathers, for example, we do not share Nell's tears or know of her 'bursting heart' until we have heard Miss Monflathers:

, you know . . . how naughty it is of you . . . to be a wax-work when you might have the proud consciousness of assisting, to extent of your infant powers, the manufactures of your country . . and of earning a comfortable and independent subsistence of from two-and-ninepence to three shillings per week? Don't you know that the harder you are at work, the happier you are?'

The brief scenes in the Black Country are also a glimpse of the outward world, though even they are in an allegorical manner: on reaching it, the child and the old man land at a dark wharf 'as if raised from the dead and placed there by a miracle'. They meet an old furnace-man, and are led within the factory where 'moving like dreams in the flame and smoke', they see men who labour 'like giants'. The language can be sharp and spare. Nell knocks at a wayside hovel:

'What would you have here?' said a gaunt miserable man opening it.
'Charity. A morsel of bread.'
'Do you see that?' returned the man hoarsely, pointing to a kind of bundle on the ground. 'That's a dead child. . . . Do you think I have charity to bestow, or a morsel of bread to spare?'

There is more in *The Old Curiosity Shop* than 'allegory' and Little Nell. In the company of Dick Swiveller, Quilp, Mrs Jarley and Sampson and Sally Brass, the clouds of sentimentality are soon blown away. There are a dozen or more characters – including Codlin and Short, the Marchioness, Mr Chuckster, and Kit Nubbles – who are wonderfully good company. The remarkable Dick Swiveller is uniquely plausible, and delightfully natural; and the transference of his devotion to the Marchioness from Sophie Wackles and Little Nell is a more satisfactory progress than any in the book.

The dwarf, Quilp, is one of the 'wild grotesque companions' who beset the path of the young heroine. In appearance and behaviour he is far removed from actual life. He is a little fiend, 'as sharp as a ferret and as cunning as a weasel'. Seated at table, 'he ate hard eggs, shell and all, devoured gigantic prawns with their heads and tails on . . . drank boiling tea without winking, bit his fork and spoon till they bent again, and in short performed so many horrifying and uncommon acts', that we have to doubt whether he is 'really a human creature'. Yet he has human vices, and even makes them seem attractive. His ferocity and spitefulness have a zest that gains him one disciple, young Tom Scott. He is sadistic, lecherous, dirty, a gibing mocker of all innocently paternal Nelly-worshippers, and represents the unrestrainedly evil side of human nature, as powerfully as the dark dwarfed figure to be released by the potions of Dr Jekyll in the tale by Robert Louis Stevenson (1850-94), *Dr Jekyll and Mr Hyde* (1886).

PLATE 4:   Quilp, by Hablot K. Browne.

The Marchioness is an attractive character, and her resourceful devotion to Dick Swiveller, who is the only person ever to have been kind to her, is more touching than Nell's to her grandfather. It is a strange thought that, in order to make some particular point, Dickens thought of making her the illegitimate daughter of Quilp and Sally Brass, but cut this from the proofs. Sampson and Sally come to a bad end, and are last seen as two wretched shadows gliding out at night through the worst haunts of the London underworld, like other terrible spectres seen in its streets, who seem 'the embodied spirits of Disease, and Vice and Famine'. It has sometimes been thought too harsh a fate for two such amusing characters, but it is the shadow of the allegory again, which they elsewhere helped to hold at bay with a band of characters as entertaining as in any of the shorter novels.

At the end of *The Old Curiosity Shop*, Master Humphrey's club is briefly revived, to allow him to take another manuscript from the clock-case and start the weekly readings again. The new story is *Barnaby Rudge, A Tale of the Riots of 'Eighty*, one Dickens had had in mind for many years. It is a novel we will deal with more briefly, though without any wish to belittle it. It was considered by the author more carefully than might be expected, but what it does best is to be found elsewhere in Dickens's novels as well. The attack on Newgate recurs in the assault on the Bastille in *A Tale of Two Cities*, and its horrific understanding of violence and cruelty is restated in other novels.

It is difficult to say how much we should make, in writing of Dickens himself, of his tremendous zest in describing scenes of uprising and revolt. He enjoyed writing them, and felt personally involved. 'I have just burst into Newgate, and am going in the next number, to tear the prisoners out by the hair of their heads', he wrote, and 'I have let all the prisoners out of Newgate . . . and played the very devil. . . I feel quite smoky when I am at work'. In a sense he was a rebel and sympathised with the rioters. Yet it was a horrified fascination; he was repelled as well as attracted; and he was well aware of his inclination. There would have been no need to explain to Dickens how a hangman, like Dennis, has a revolting attractiveness: he even wrote a special article on the subject a few years later, when he read letters applying for the post of hangman when an official vacancy was announced ('The Finishing Schoolmaster', *Household Words*, 17 May 1851). He understood the strange attraction of violence: how 'sober workmen going home from their day's labour' become 'rioters in an instant', and how drink and violence may turn men into 'fiends', 'wolves' and 'wild animals'. No one knew better how the 'appetite and love for the marvellous and terrible' are 'among the natural characteristics of mankind' (Chapter 54). The madness of Barnaby and Lord George, and the outrages of the mob composed of ordinary men, are all on the shadow-line of sanity and insanity.

His sympathy with the rebel was part of his exasperation at repression in society. For it is as true of *Barnaby Rudge* as of his next novel that its social message is 'As we sow, we reap', and it is powerfully expressed. Dickens was to declare that 'from every seed of evil . . . a field of ruin is grown. . . . There is no people on earth it would not put to shame'. While he was engaged on the work he wrote to the novelist Mrs Catherine Frances Gore (1799-1861) of the children of the city streets, 'I have seen in London whenever I walk alone into its bye ways at night, as I often do, such miseries and horrors among these little creatures – such an impossibility of their ever growing up to be good and happy – that those aristocratic dolls do turn me sick'. In a similar way he wrote to another correspondent that he meant 'to pursue cruelty and oppression . . . so long as I have energy of thought and the power of giving it utterance'.

When the American writer Edgar Allan Poe (1809-49) reviewed it he fussed excessively over the plot but praised Dickens's power of creating atmosphere and his 'intuitive feeling for the forcible and true which is the *sixth sense* of a man of genius'. It was a work in which Dickens developed his ability to use melodrama to image forces he would have found it hard to analyse. From recognising man's love of the 'marvellous and terrible', Dickens was learning to use it to show conflicts within man and society.

While at work on the novel Dickens and his wife had visited Scotland where he made a great impression in Edinburgh. As it drew to a close he began to have greater ambitions as a traveller; and shortly before completing the book he announced to his readers: 'Taking advantage of the respite which the close of this work will afford me, I have decided, in January next, to pay a visit to America.'

Chapter 6

America, 1842;
Martin Chuzzlewit

Once decided on America Dickens lost no time. Catherine was to go with him, arrangements were made for the children to stay behind, and berths booked on the steamship *Britannia*, due to leave Liverpool early in January 1842. Even a serious illness could not blight his enthusiasm. America, he said, he had already visited in 'day-dreams many times', he 'yearned to know' its people, and far from disapproving of republicanism he had every sympathy for the revolution provoked by the 'obstinacy of that swine-headed anointed of the Lord – his Majesty King George the Third'.

The crossing was terrible. Catherine wrote to her sister:

> You cannot imagine what a dreadful Voyage we had. We were 18 days in our passage and experienced all the horror of a storm at Sea. . . . I was nearly distracted with terror and don't know what I should have done, had it not been for the great kindness and composure of my dear Charles. . . . We met another danger . . . after that. Owing to our unskilful Pilot we ran aground which caused great consternation as we were surrounded by rocks. . . . We were told, after the danger was past, that the sailors had taken off their jackets and shoes ready to swim ashore.

All through their travels Catherine loyally put up with all kinds of hardships without complaint, leaving the limelight to her husband and thinking chiefly of the children she had left behind.

At Boston they were met by reporters, who 'came leaping on board at peril of their lives', and for whom Dickens felt an instinctive revulsion. But other first impressions were favourable. The hotel was 'excellent', and 'good nature, universal'. There were letters of welcome from the authorities of almost every State, deputations from the Far West, and invitations to all kinds of entertainments. 'There was never king or emperor,' he wrote, 'so cheered or followed by crowds.' He worked hard at getting to know the country and its institutions; and, a week after their arrival, they attended a banquet which was the climax of the reception at Boston. 'It was a most superb affair,' Dickens told Forster, 'and the speaking *admirable*. Indeed, the general talent for public speaking here is . . . most striking.' He made his own mark in a speech in which he told how he had 'dreamed by day and night for years of setting foot upon this shore', and how even if he had come there 'unknowing and unknown', it would have been with 'all my sympathies clustering richly round this land and people', and 'all my energies as fully bent on judging for myself, and speaking out, and telling in my sphere the truth, as I do now when you rain down welcomes on my head'.

From Boston they went to Hartford, where he enjoyed a visit to a lunatic asylum and being serenaded by a college choir. But the harmony between Dickens and his hosts was soon broken. Near the end of his speech at Boston, he had briefly mentioned international copyright, and at Hartford he committed the same offence. After the dinner, speech followed speech as toasts were given to 'A Common Language and Literature', 'The Great Republic of Letters', and 'Literature – that Neutral Ground on which Men of Every Clime meet in Peaceful Homage to the Intellect'; but Dickens could not help thinking that in spite of a common literature, America contributed little to it financially, and that it was neutral ground only if certain delicate topics were avoided.

Dickens's strength (and weakness) as a traveller in America, was that he tended to judge everything in terms of right or wrong. He was like one of his own heroes, who could not 'stand by' and see injustice done. So, when he replied, after thanking his listeners, he said that though it is always difficult to judge an author's 'personal character from his writings', he thought that at least 'a reader will rise from the perusal of a book with some defined . . . idea of the writer's moral creed and broad purposes'. He went on: 'Gentlemen, my moral creed . . . is very easily summed up. . . . I take it that we are born and that we hold our sympathies, hopes and energies in trust for the many, and not for the few. That we cannot hold in too strong a light of disgust and contempt . . . all meanness, falsehood, cruelty and oppression. . . . Above all, that nothing is high, because it is in a high place; and that nothing is low because it is in a low one.' After further compliments, he came to the point by saying: 'Gentlemen, as I have no secrets from you, in the spirit of the confidence you have engendered between us . . . I would beg leave to whisper in your ear two words, *International Copyright.*'

He reminded them that books by British authors were reprinted in America without any payment to the writers, which most of them badly needed; that American authors suffered even more, since even at home they could be paid little as long as foreign works could be had for nothing; and that, as a speaker at Boston had said, if there had been an international copyright agreement in the past, 'Scott might not have sunk beneath the mighty pressure on his brain'. Like Captain

Frederick Marryat (1792-1848) and Harriet Martineau (1802-76), both travellers in the United States before him, Dickens would not acquiesce in American piracy; and though he did not directly link his belief in a 'moral creed' with the need for international copyright, it was clear that he made the connection.

No worse time could have been chosen for raising the question. Not that either British or American authors had allowed it to drop, but it was unwise to mention it in public. During the past few years 'mammoth' newspapers had arisen, in which the most popular new works were published for a few cents. Almost all American writers agreed with Dickens and wanted a copyright agreement; but in attacking piracy Dickens was attacking the press, and the American press was to hit back by any means, fair or foul. No time was lost. *The Hartford Daily Times*, reporting the speech, ominously remarked of international copyright: 'It happens that we want no advice upon this subject, and it will be better for Mr. Dickens, if he refrains from introducing the matter.'

Dickens was not to be put off. He kept to an energetic programme of visiting all kinds of public institutions, from schools to prisons, and at New York, he and Catherine attended a tremendous reception, known as the 'Boz Ball'. But when arrangements were made for another banquet in his honour he told the committee that he felt bound to speak on international copyright, and (as he wrote to Forster) 'nothing should deter me . . . and that as I would not spare them when I got home, I would not be silent here'.

At the dinner the chair was taken by Washington Irving, whose essays Dickens liked almost as much as those of Oliver Goldsmith and who admired Dickens in return. After reading *The Old Curiosity Shop*, Irving had written to Dickens to persuade him to come to America. In fact, as a speaker, he was inaudible, but Dickens rose to the occasion. He said that he meant it to be his last public speech in America, 'for remembering the short time I have before me in this land of mighty interest . . . I have felt it almost a duty to decline the honours which my generous friends elsewhere would heap upon me, and . . . to pass through the country more quietly'. He expressed gratitude 'with a full heart', and declared that he would always have 'a deeper sense' of their 'kind, affectionate and noble greeting', than it was 'possible to convey', and very moderately spoke about copyright in public for the last time.

To understand Dickens's reason for persistently bringing the matter forward, it should be appreciated that he was now Britain's foremost *professional* author, who deliberately set himself to do all he could to raise the standard of his profession. *Pickwick* had been dedicated to T. N. Talfourd as the author of the British Copyright Bill; *Nickleby* attacked dramatic pirates, and contained several shrewd asides on the 'dignity' of the profession; and, though Dickens had a personal interest as well, he was a spokesman for others.

Their travels continued, on to the cities of Philadelphia and Washington; to Richmond, Pittsburgh, Cincinnati, and down the Ohio as far as St Louis. Where the Ohio joins the Mississippi, they passed the city of Cairo, to re-appear in *Chuzzlewit* as Eden, which 'the waters of the Deluge might have left . . . but a week before, so choked with slime and matted growth was the hideous swamp which bore that name'.

As they went on, his opinions changed. He was disillusioned by what he heard about Washington, and even more by what he saw. Some of his most outspoken letters were written to Macready, who was strongly pro-American – just as he himself had been before he came. 'It's no use,' he wrote, 'I am disappointed. This is not the republic I came to see; this is not the republic of my imagination.' He wrote again:

> I have not changed – I cannot change . . . – my secret opinion of this country. . . I believe the heaviest blow ever dealt at Liberty's Head, will be dealt by this nation in the ultimate failure of its example to the Earth. See what is passing now – Look at the exhausted Treasury; the paralyzed Government; the unworthy representatives of a free people; the desperate contests between the North and the South; the iron curb and brazen muzzle fastened on every man who speaks his mind, even in that Republican Hall, to which Republican men are sent by a Republican people to speak Republican Truths – the stabbings and the shootings, and coarse and really brutal threatenings exchanged between Senators under the very Senate's roof – the intrusion of the most pitiful, mean, malicious, creeping crawling party spirit, into all transactions of life . . . the silly, drivelling, slandering, wicked, monstrous, Party Press . . . .
>
> P.S. I need not say that I have many pleasant things to say of America . . . I speak to you as I would to myself. I am a Lover of Freedom, disappointed. – That's all.

Much of his visit he enjoyed, and he made many friends who stood by him even after he had published *American Notes* and *Martin Chuzzlewit*. But the whole visit was poisoned by attacks in the press. A few days after the speech in New York, he wrote privately to the Mayor of Boston to say that they gave him 'agony such as I have never experienced'. He kept this from Catherine but, as he warned Macready after reaching home, 'if you knew but one hundredth part of the malignity, the monstrous falsehood, the beastly attacks made even upon Catherine, which were published all over America . . . on my mere confession that the country had disappointed me – confessions wrung from me in private society before I had written a word', he would not question his opinion. Already, Dickens told the Mayor, scores of newspapers had attacked him 'in such terms of vagabond scurrility as they would denounce no murderer with'.

No one has fully investigated this, partially or impartially. No doubt Dickens exaggerated. But it is clear that he was bitterly hurt. More than most men, at this time of his life, Dickens was dependent on establishing friendly relations with his public. He had come to America with 'all his sympathies clustering richly round its lands and people', and now he found this affection blasted by men he could only see as enemies. It was by no means only British visitors who found the American press personal, vindictive and irresponsible; and he was caught, for example, between the spicy vulgarities of the *New York Herald* and the moral belligerence of the *Washington Globe*, which wrote that:

> If to delineate the human character in its lowest state of ignorance, vice and degradation . . . is to be a Democratic writer, then most assuredly Mr Dickens is one. He had exhibited human nature in its naked, ragged, deformity, reeking with vice and pollution. . . . Such a school of literature can only aid the course and progress of vice.

It seems clear, too, that Dickens was driven to keep within rather a limited circle of friends and supporters, and that in his outspoken hatred of slavery he put another barrier between himself and public opinion. He had meant to be quiet about it, but, when questioned directly, spoke out.

They continued their tour by stage-coach, steamer, and railway, seeing more of the people when away from the cities – too much sometimes – and finding them 'frank, brave, cordial, hospitable and affectionate'. Yet Dickens preferred educated Americans, whose 'cultivation and refinement . . . enhance their warmth of heart and ardent enthusiasm'. But it was with relief that they passed into Canada, where he 'was taken dreadfully loyal after dinner, and drank the Queen's health in a bumper'. They spent a month there, taking part in some amateur theatricals at Montreal, returned to New York on 6 June, and sailed for England.

He quickly settled to writing the travel book. He had always meant to do this to pay expenses, and his letters to Forster were meant as a record to work from on return. Even before his return, Forster had been reading from them to select friends; Bulwer Lytton enjoyed them, writing: 'I have been haunted by visions of the "Piazza" commemorated by Dickens. How Swift would have smiled and revelled!'; and Henry Crabb Robinson (1775-1867), the diarist and writer, remarked, 'I went after breakfast . . . to Forster's to hear him read. . . . Better letters I never heard. . . . The descriptions most animated, satire and sublime painting admirably intermixed. I was gratified by finding that he had not been deceived by the gross flattery of the people. He confirms my dislike. . . . Their want of honesty is not so flagrant as their grossness of manners, but it is as certain'.

Yet once he had gathered his letters home Dickens took care to leave out all personal references, all satire, in fact nearly everything that made his letters to Forster so entertaining. In later years, before they were destroyed, Forster went to the length of having a lock fitted to the letters after they were bound. The actual *American Notes* appear pleasantly innocuous. Dickens even wrote a preface, later suppressed, explaining that his book was 'not statistical . . . comprehends no small talk . . . has not a grain of political ingredient, nor any lengthened or minute account of my personal reception. . . . This book is simply what it claims to be – a record of the impressions I received from day to day, during my hasty travels in America'. Nevertheless it is possibly the best American travel-book of the period: none other comes up to it.

Bitterness about copyright rankled on both sides, and Dickens tried to encourage British protest, but it was a hopeless cause. Meanwhile the newspaper war continued, letters were forged and printed over Dickens's name, and letters criticising Dickens supposedly signed by prominent men such as the Irish nationalist leader Daniel O'Connell (1775-1847) were added to them. In fact, O'Connell joined Dickens in referring to 'the vileness of a great portion of the newspaper press in the United States'. Forster rashly stoked the fire with two long anonymous articles in the *Foreign Quarterly Review*, promptly and maliciously attributed to Dickens. So far as studying *Martin Chuzzlewit* goes, it is of interest mainly because it reminds us that while Dickens's satire may speak for itself, here it was pointedly aimed at an actual society.

Many Americans shrugged off the accustomed press abuse. Others sympathised. Dickens wrote to his friend the American poet Henry Wadsworth Longfellow (1807-82) of another forgery, 'You know what the American press is, and will be, I dare say, as little surprised at this outrage as I was'. One of the examples Forster selected to show the Americans' fear of their own press was the recent notorious Somers case, of the execution of a midshipman by his pious commander, which was to give the American novelist Herman Melville (1819-91) the idea for Captain Vere and *Billy Budd*. But it was left to Dickens to speak out.

As soon as he had finished *American Notes*, he was off on an uproarious Cornish holiday with some friends. 'I have never laughed in my life as I did on this journey; seriously, I do not believe there ever was such a trip.' Once back he began work telling Forster, 'Behold finally, the title of the new book. . . . "The Life and Adventures of Martin Chuzzlewit, his family, friends, and enemies"'.

The book was in monthly numbers because he had found weekly serialisation 'anxious, perplexing, and difficult', but it was still hard to start. He shut himself up 'for days . . . without writing a word', and replied half-jokingly to a friend about being 'in the agonies of contriving and planning . . . in which stage I am accustomed to walk up and down the house, smiting my head dejectedly, and to be so horribly cross that the boldest fly at my approach'. It was with a 'Thank God!' that he announced that the first number was nearly finished.

It was on sale in January 1843, as Dickens went 'hammering away' at future numbers. Yet it was not long before he learnt that it was selling worse than any of his previous novels: the opening was obscure, the public seemed to be taking him for granted, the material was unsuitable for the family, and once a serial made a bad start it was hard to recover. Matters went so far that one of the partners of Chapman & Hall proposed halving Dickens's usual monthly payments. At this he declared that when the work was finished he would break with them. 'You know as well as I,' he told Forster, 'that I think *Chuzzlewit* . . . immeasurably the best of my stories.' In the long run his confidence was justified. For the present he was 'so irritated, so rubbed in the tenderest part of my eye-lids with bay-salt', that he was almost unable to write.

Yet *Chuzzlewit* has numerous weaknesses, among them being the plot, the worse for its ambition to weave a mystery round the curmudgeonly old Martin who is finally transformed into a universal benefactor. Its closing scene is a triumph of theatrical conventionality which would have shamed Vincent Crummles. It is true that, after he had finished, Dickens said that he had tried 'to resist the temptation of the current Monthly Number, and to keep a steadier eye on the general purpose and design' (Preface), but this is not evident in the story. True, too, that the manuscript shows that from the end of the third number he had already decided on 'Old Martin's plot to degrade and punish Pecksniff in the end'. Yet it is not well worked out.

The best things in the novel, in fact, were not planned, but grew. The development of Pecksniff's character especially was unforeseen. 'As to the way in which these characters have opened out,' Dickens wrote, 'that is to me one of the most surprising processes of the mind in this sort of invention. Given what one knows, what one does not know springs up; and I am as absolutely certain of its being true, as I am of the law of gravitation – if such a thing be possible, more so.' Such, Forster says revealingly, 'was the very process of creation', with all important characters. Both Mrs Gamp and Pecksniff were founded on real people, and, given what he knew of them, Dickens felt that almost by a natural law he could show what they could say or do in any possible circumstances.

Pecksniff himself derived from a prolific writer on a variety of subjects, Samuel Carter Hall (1800-89) – 'Shirt-collar Hall', as the journalist Douglas Jerrold (1803-57) called him – and, to leave no doubt, he was introduced as 'A most exemplary man. . . . His very throat was moral. You saw a good deal of it. You looked over a very low fence of white cravat . . . and there it lay, a valley between two jutting heights of collar, serene and whiskerless before you'. Hall had a reputation like Pecksniff's, and, for Dickens's taste, he may even have had too grovelling a liking for Americans. Writing to his friend and fellow novelist Wilkie Collins (1824-89) about a Fourth of July dinner to celebrate American independence, Dickens still found him loathsome enough, even thirteen years later, for his 'bile' to 'begin to shake and swell, like Green's balloon with the gas turned on. . . . Being on the Salt Sea you probably did not see a speech of Samivel Carter Hall's. . . . The snivelling insolence of it, the concentrated essence of Snobbery' and its 'Philogullododgeitiveness'.

But for Forster's authority we might have thought that when Dickens began to write the novel, he had it already in his mind to show that selfishness and low cunning have their place on both sides of the Atlantic. Yet his decision to send Martin to America may have been taken as suddenly as his hero's. Once there, the moral theme flourishes once more: 'Pecksniff's house was more than a thousand miles away; and again this happy chronicle has Liberty and Moral Sensibility for its high companions.' If hypocrisy, as the French critic Hippolyte Taine (1828-93) said, was the English vice, then it had become naturalised in the United States. In fact, 'if native statesmen, orators, and pamphleteers are to be believed,' said Dickens, 'that peculiarly transatlantic article, a moral sense' had been quite monopolised in America. The satire of the New York Norrises is based on the fact that they are just like their counterparts in England, and that, as the 'good' American Mr Bevan remarks, 'they are made of pretty much the same stuff as other folks, if they would but own it, and not set up on false pretences'.

No justice can be done to the satire of the other American characters in a few sentences. Unfair it may be, but there is a relish about the way Dickens lays on the lash, which is unmatched in his work elsewhere. Washington Irving, who had wept when Dickens left, refused to meet him again. The resentment of the poet William Cullen Bryant (1794-1878) lasted till Dickens's return to America in 1867 when he would neither see him nor go to one of the readings. It was not so much that they objected to his satire of their fellow-countrymen like Hannibal

Chollop, Jefferson Brick and Elijah Pogram, but that they could not forgive the insults to their country: 'That Republic, but yesterday let loose upon her noble course, and . . . to-day so maimed and lame, so full of sores and ulcers . . . that her best friends turn from the loathsome creature with disgust.' Nor did they feel the book unjust so much as exaggerated: the people described were not representative. According to Forster, 'as time moved on . . . the laughter on their side of the Atlantic became quite as great as the amusement on our side' – a very doubtful statement.

The novel is partly held together by its moral purpose, on the theme of self. How far we can still be bothered about Dickens's moral purpose in connection with any of his novels, has sometimes been questioned. It can be taken for granted or dismissed. But if it were dismissed, the books would fall apart. They depend on an appeal to our feelings, using a rhetoric of irony and sympathy to support it. And while Dickens may sometimes write elsewhere as if our virtues were 'natural', the theme of *Martin Chuzzlewit* should not be forgotten; he is certainly clear that there is no happy return to an 'Eden' through Martin's passage to America. 'Natural' man in the Far West is as repulsive as he is in slightly more civilised forms at home. Yet it was playing a dangerous game to set up the absurdly virtuous Pinch against Pecksniff, to promote young Martin's change of heart, dwell on the insipid innocence of Ruth Pinch and Mary Graham, and to involve them all with Jonas's fearsome murder, and the raw satire of the two nations in England and America. Nor is the morality by any means conventional when it can delight us with Pecksniff and Mrs Gamp, whose likeable absurdities are human rather than grotesque.

The novel is also held together by Dickens's vital energy, his highly sententious if often vulgar commentary, and his sense of the intoxication in life, its menace and Gothic horrors. Throughout they are all shown with a hallucinatory effect, expressed most powerfully in Jonas's desperate act of murder. The night before, the victim (Tigg) has a nightmare of trying to bar his bedroom door, working 'with iron plates and nails to make the door secure; but . . . the nails broke, or changed to soft twigs, or what was worse to worms . . . and the iron plates curled up like hot paper'. After killing Tigg, Jonas returns home to his 'blotched, stained, mouldering room, like a vault', with the pipes running through it that unexpectedly 'clicked and gurgled suddenly as if they were choking', and he hears 'his own heart beating Murder, Murder, Murder'.

In spite of the book's disappointing reception, Dickens had not lost faith in his genius. 'I *know*,' he wrote, 'that I could sustain my place . . . though fifty writers started up tomorrow.' He exulted in his new skill at suggesting character. From this time forward, especially, he had the ability to show repressed feelings, which may impart a grotesque or humorous oddity, or an impression of malignant power. There is Charity Pecksniff with her thwarted hatred of Jonas; Mrs Gamp and her hideous desire to 'lay out' one of her patients, a handsome young man, as a corpse; the more vicious Americans; and Pecksniff's hilariously drunken oratory after the dinner-party at Todgers's which Dickens painfully self-censored in manuscript. It was Carlyle who said that 'in every man there is a madman', and having discovered this for himself, Dickens develops the idea in his works.

Chapter 7

Christmas Books and *Dombey and Son*

Chuzzlewit was dedicated 'To Miss Burdett Coutts . . . With the True and Earnest Regard of the Author'. She was one of the daughters of Sir Francis Burdett, and had recently inherited the name and fortune of her grandfather, Thomas Coutts, a banker. At this time she was aged thirty and had known Dickens for about five years. She was a strange woman. During the first part of her life she was a devoted philanthropist, using her fortune for all kinds of good works, personal charity, Church endowments and useful social experiments. Once she and Dickens had become friends he helped to administer her charities and suggested various practical schemes. Though she eventually came to be a woman of strong resolution and acquired a great reputation as a philanthropist, she was reserved and cautiously dependent on others, owing her eminence to her long life (1814-1906), a sense of duty and great wealth.

She was also a good friend, and a woman of ready sympathy. Once she and Dickens knew each other, they happily settled down to a working partnership in all kinds of schemes to help the poor in London. Their association was romantic purely in the sense that an heiress and an author worked together for almost twenty years for the good of others. We sometimes share a 'myth' of our own about bankers of the mid-nineteenth century; but, so far as Dickens was concerned (though no doubt aware of its limitations) this heiress to a banking fortune stood for a view of charity that was not entirely confined to fiction.

The first time they joined forces in anything but private charity, was in support for the first of the Ragged Schools. This was an educational movement started to help the poorest and dirtiest street-children whom no other school would take. Dickens saw a newspaper announcement, visited the school in the squalid district he had once chosen for Fagin's academy, and then wrote 'a sledge-hammer account' to Miss Coutts. Another report on the same district is given in a startling letter Dickens sent to the *Daily News* in 1846, in which he spoke of its children as 'young thieves and beggars – with nothing natural to youth about them: with nothing frank, ingenuous, or pleasant in their faces; low-browed, vicious, cunning, wicked; abandoned of all help . . . speeding downward to destruction; and UNUTTERABLY IGNORANT'.

Aware that Miss Coutts had just given two hundred pounds to a Church subscription list, Dickens persuaded her to pay for a bathhouse for the school and to give other kinds of practical assistance. He wanted this assistance to be given with the stipulation that there should be no narrow-minded or merely religious teaching in its classes, and, confident that Miss Coutts would do as he recommended, he enthusiastically wrote: 'She is a most excellent creature . . . and I have the most perfect affection and respect for her.'

Though he already knew about the need for such work, the sight of the Ragged Schools seems to have given a stimulus to another book started 'in the odd moments of leisure left him by *Chuzzlewit*'. Again it was something completely new, nothing less than *A Christmas Carol*. It was meant to be in the fashion of old nursery tales; and, once he had started on it, so Dickens wrote, he 'excited himself in the most extraordinary manner' in writing it, walking 'the black streets of London' thinking of it, 'fifteen and twenty miles many a night when all the sober folks had gone to bed'.

To some modern tastes the transformation of Scrooge may have begun to cloy; but this should not stop us from seeing the ingenuity of the *Carol*'s construction, and its unflagging vitality. The later Christmas books, except *The Chimes*, show every sign of being written to order, but *A Christmas Carol* is spontaneous. It is not all mistletoe, good cheer and Christmas pudding. The young thieves and beggars of Field Lane reappear just as the Ghost of Christmas Present is about to leave:

'Spirit! are they yours?' Scrooge could say no more.

'They are Man's,' said the Spirit, looking down upon them. 'And they cling to me appealing from their fathers. This boy is Ignorance. This girl is Want. Beware them both' . . . .

'Have they no refuge or resource?' cried Scrooge.

'Are there no prisons?' said the Spirit, turning on him . . . with his own words. 'Are there no workhouses?'

The bell struck twelve.

Scrooge looked about him for the Ghost, and saw it not.

Even in *A Christmas Carol* Dickens expresses much more than what the French critic Louis Cazamian called a mere 'philosophie de Noël'. It is true that the main emphasis is on pious benevolence; but *A Christmas Carol* is not just a cry for a change of heart: the warning to beware Want and Ignorance is not less memorable than Tiny Tim's 'God bless Us Every One!'

It made an instant sensation. Lord Jeffrey thought it had 'done more good' than could be 'traced to all the pulpits and confessionals in Christendom' during the past year. Thackeray declared it 'a national benefit', and Dickens told Macready that it was his 'most prodigious success'. Unhappily it was financially disappointing. For, still struggling to be independent of publishers, he had persuaded Chapman & Hall to bring it out purely on commission, hoping to gain all the profits himself. But it was too expensively produced, and, after his disagreements with Chapman & Hall over *Chuzzlewit*, Dickens found new publishers. They were Bradbury & Evans, whom he kept till after 1858 when he returned to Chapman & Hall.

He was altogether unsettled, and decided to live abroad for a while. He was still not happy about publishing in monthly parts, and there were times when he was almost appalled at writing so much. He had tried the escape of going to America; had started the *Clock* to avoid writing fiction; had even unsuccessfully applied to a member of the Government to appoint him a paid London magistrate like Henry Fielding; and now he decided to take a year in Italy. He was haunted by the fate of Sir Walter Scott, who saw Italy only in old age when he was 'a driveller in his miserable decay'.

In a few months' time, Dickens gathered up his family, packed it into an enormous 'old shabby devil of a coach', and set off. At Lyons they went down the Rhône, and at Marseilles embarked for Genoa. On arrival they settled into the Villa di Bella Vista, a 'lonely, rusty, stagnant staggerer of a domain'. It was summer. The Alps ranged in the distance, the sea was a vivid Prussian blue, and the vineyards below were 'green, green, green'. It suited Dickens, who gaily wrote: 'The day gets brighter, brighter, brighter till it's night. The summer gets hotter, hotter, hotter till it explodes. The fruit gets riper, riper, riper till it tumbles down and rots.' He entered into the spirit of Italy, and wrote home another series of letters for a book.

After a month or more they moved into the Palazzo Peschiere, where Dickens began his second Christmas book. He had possibly been disappointed that readers had taken to heart only the more comforting passages of the *Carol*, and this time meant to write to 'shame the cruel and canting'. At first he longed for the familiar London streets, and wrote that he had never so staggered on 'the threshold' of a book before. The clash of steeple bells set his brain reeling. Then, suddenly, Forster received a note which said, 'We have heard THE CHIMES at midnight, Master Shallow!' and he knew that his friend had found the title.

Now, while unsettled by these difficulties, when convent bells were sounding through the night, and he was sleeping in a strange room where mass had often been performed, Dickens had an extraordinary recurrence of dreams about Mary Hogarth. This may not seem surprising, but the way he describes it shows that it seemed as startling as a vision, and 'as real, animated, and full of passion as Macready . . . in the last scene of *Macbeth*'. Mary's spirit appeared 'in blue drapery', like a Raphael Madonna:

> It was so full of compassion and sorrow for me . . . that it cut me to the heart. . . . I said, in an agony of entreaty lest it should leave me, 'What is the True religion?' As it paused a moment . . . I said . . . in such an agony of haste, lest it should go away! – 'You think, as I do, that the Form of religion does not so greatly matter, if we try to do good? – or,' I said . . . 'perhaps the Roman Catholic is the best?' . . . 'For *you*,' said the Spirit, full of such heavenly tenderness for me, that I felt as if my heart would break, 'for *you*, it is the best!' Then I awoke, with the tears running down my face, and myself in exactly the condition of the dream.

Its importance may lie in what it suggests of the depth of Dickens's feelings. So natural in all other ways, he was unlike almost anyone else in his intensity. Forster, in fact, says that he had recently suffered doubts and difficulties about religion, and that this was the first thought 'that would have risen' in connection with the dream, 'in any mind to which his was intimately known'. This is important, though not to be found elsewhere in Dickens's letters or recorded conversations. The dream certainly did not come from a leaning to Roman Catholicism, of which he deeply disapproved. It was probably influenced by the natural association of Mary's name and the Virgin: not new to Dickens if we remember that on the headboard of Little Nell's death-bed (also associated with Mary Hogarth) Dickens's illustrator had pictured the Virgin.

There were no more developments. The incident passed, and Dickens turned his attention to the supernatural machinery of *The Chimes*. Possibly his liking for getting over narrative difficulties in his stories in this way, is partly explained by his extraordinary power of seeing imaginary figures as if they were real, and of giving inanimate objects some of his own vitality. In outline, his new tale was just an account of Trotty Veck, an old messenger or ticket-porter, who has a horrifying vision of his daughter's future from which he prays to the Spirits of the Bells to save her. Though not among his best works, in some ways it brings us close to Dickens. Forster says that its 'intensity . . . seemed always best to represent to himself what he hoped to be longest remembered for', and that to the last it had 'a cherished corner' in his heart.

Clearly it grew out of his deeper thinking about the causes of social injustice and enmity between rich and poor, and was an appeal to break down the barriers of prejudice that existed between classes, and to affirm man's common humanity. It was largely provoked by what Dickens read in the newspapers, at home and abroad, and in particular by a statement made by Sir Peter Laurie (1779-1861), a magistrate and former lord mayor (Alderman Cute in *The Chimes*), who threatened to 'put down' would-be suicides by severe punishment if any more were brought before him.

The final pathetic scene, in which Trotty imagines that his daughter is about to leap into the Thames with her child in her arms, rather than bring her up to a life of shame, was suggested by the same incident that inspired Thomas Hood's 'The Bridge of Sighs'. After desperate suffering, a woman called Mary Furley jumped into the river, with her two children. She and one child had been saved; the other was drowned. She was tried for murder, and sentenced to death with some relish by a judge who added various remarks about her 'premeditated cruelty', and the certainty of her execution. Of course she was reprieved; but the report of her trial made a great stir at the time, though now completely forgotten.

Such characters and scenes as these were topical, and so were some others: the rick-burner, Will Fern, the political economist, Mr Filer, and the pompous and patronising Tory philanthropist, Sir Joseph Bowley, drawn with the great philanthropist Lord Shaftesbury (1801-85) in mind. Composing the story left Dickens 'hot and giddy', with large eyes, lank hair and a swollen face. 'I wouldn't write it twice for something,' he told Forster. By the time he had finished, he was feverish with work, but intensely proud of what he had done.

Nothing would suit him but to return to London. He had to see *The Chimes* through the press, and even more he wanted to try out its effect. He dashed off to see more of Italy, and then returned to England, which he reached at the end of November. Forster collected a small audience for him including Thomas Carlyle, Daniel Maclise, Douglas Jerrold, and several other well-known men, and Dickens read aloud to them. 'If you had seen Macready,' he wrote to Catherine, 'undisguisedly sobbing and crying on the sofa . . . you would have felt, as I did, what a thing it is to have power.' Maclise also wrote to Catherine: 'You will never be able to conceive the effect. . . . We should borrow the high language of the minor theatre and even then not do the effect justice – shrieks of laughter – there were indeed – and floods of tears. . . . I do not think there was ever such a triumphant hour for Charles.'

Dickens then returned to spend Christmas with his family, and the whole caravan was got on the move for Rome. While there he continued sending descriptions home, which were published first in the *Daily News* as 'Travelling Sketches – Written on the Road', and later, in book form, in 1846 as *Pictures from Italy*. 'It is a great pleasure to me,' he told Forster, 'to find that you are pleased with these shadows in water.'

By the end of May 1845 they were home, and once again Dickens engaged in a whirl of activities. He took to amateur theatricals, and produced *Every Man in His Humour* (1598) by Ben Jonson (1573-1637) and began thinking of his next Christmas book, *The Cricket on the Hearth*. There were two more after this, *The Battle of Life* (1846) and *The Haunted Man* (1848), before he saw they were losing their spontaneity by becoming a habit. Even so, they were useful as experiments in literary technique by encouraging him to compress the narration through contrivances such as the use of key phrases and rather obvious allegory. Yet they were spoiled by being written with one eye on dramatic adaptation. His novels were possibly less obviously affected by his love of drama than often supposed; but later Christmas books are ruined by an exaggerated concern for their reappearance on the stage.

Far more exciting, for the moment, was an invitation to join in founding a new national daily paper. Dickens had been hankering to do something of the kind ever since he was established as a novelist. He still wanted a regular salary, and he would have dearly liked to be able to use the press as an agency to agitate for all kinds of liberal reforms with which the novels could deal only indirectly. Here was the chance to be editor of a Liberal newspaper, at the height of the battle for Free Trade and the repeal of the Corn laws, the hated tax on imported grain. He could staff it as he wished, and be largely responsible for its policy. In spite of his friends' misgivings, he threw himself into the business heart and soul, in partnership with Bradbury & Evans and certain railway capitalists who also wanted to influence public opinion.

Just what went wrong it is hard to say. The first number of the *Daily News* was published on 21 January 1846. By 30 January, Dickens was talking of handing in his resignation, and by 9 February it had been accepted. Though some time afterwards (in the preface to *Pictures from Italy*) he referred to it all as 'a brief mistake', he worked extremely hard to set the paper going. It seems that he did not get on well with other directors, disliked the irregular hours and routine drudgery, feared the influence of its financial backers, and realised that he was not the man for the job. It is unfair to blame either Dickens or his partners. At any rate, Forster took his place and, after further difficulties, the paper was safely launched.

Once free, Dickens took up the idea of a new monthly serial. At the same time he decided to live abroad for a year, where he could concentrate on writing. He fixed on Lausanne and, by June, had set off with his wife, six children and Georgina Hogarth. They rented a little house called Rosemont, with 'roses enough to smother the whole establishment of the *Daily News*', and made friends with a pleasant circle of English residents. Then, at last, he started, writing: 'BEGAN

DOMBEY! – I performed this feat yesterday . . . and it is a plunge straight over head and ears into the story.'

Despite this description of plunging headlong into the story Dickens thought out *Dombey and Son* in advance as intensely as he did any of his books. Of all Dickens's novels it most easily shows how the story and structure were planned and grew. The idea had originated early in the year, and since then Dickens had been brooding over it, and thinking out its design carefully. Just before he took the house at Lausanne, he had decided that it would be better to spend the winter in Paris, by which time he meant to have written four numbers and have reached the point in the story 'when the life and crowd of that extraordinary place will come vividly to my assistance in writing'. This clearly suggests that, even before he had put pen to paper, he had thought out the number-division of at least the first part of the book.

Years later, an account of Dickens's usual methods was given by one of his publishers, Frederic Chapman. In an interview with a reporter (*Daily Chronicle*, 25 June 1892) he stressed Dickens's care for what he wrote. He commented on Dickens's way with manuscript and proofs, and how 'up to the very moment of the appearance of the book', he took and extremely active part in correcting and changing it, and then explained that when Dickens began on a novel he first got 'hold of a central idea', which he 'revolved in his mind until he had thought the matter thoroughly out'. Finally he 'made what I might call a programme of his story with the characters', and 'upon this skeleton story he set to work and gave it literary sinew, blood and life'.

Chapman's account reminds us that in all Dickens's later works, at least, there is a central idea, kept in mind while the plot is developed, and the fact that there is such a 'central idea' in every work from *Martin Chuzzlewit* onwards, clearly distinguishes the later novels from the earlier.

As well as this, in writing *Dombey*, Dickens began to draw up in detail a series of what are known as his 'part-' or 'number-plans'. No doubt these are what Chapman meant when he spoke of his 'programme' or 'skeleton story'. They have been preserved, and all have the same arrangement. Dickens used to take a separate sheet of paper for each monthly number, and fold it in two. On the right-hand side he wrote down what he thought were the necessary chapter-divisions; and, on the left, he used to jot notes on the possible development of the story. He then usually filled in entries on the right-hand side, so that he knew what was to be done (or had a record of what he had done) in each chapter. Chapman was wrong only in suggesting that the whole 'skeleton' was completed in advance. It was built up number by number, and the complete design largely depended on the 'central idea', which existed only in Dickens's mind. But though the over-all plan was never formally set down on paper, we know it was well thought out in advance.

In *Dombey* there can be no doubt about this, for not only can we see that the story follows a plan, but we also know that Dickens wrote a letter to Forster explaining his intentions which he sent with the manuscript of the first number. From the first chapter Forster could learn that Dombey was a wealthy London merchant, who believed that 'the earth was made for Dombey and Son to trade in, and the sun and moon to give them light'; and from the first page he found that the story began with the birth of 'Son'. Before Dickens left England he had already explained that part of the 'central idea' of the novel was that it 'should do with Pride what its predecessor (*Chuzzlewit*) had done with Selfishness'; and he now explained his intention in much greater detail in letters:

> I design to show Mr D. with that one idea of the Son taking firmer and firmer possession of him, and swelling and bloating his pride to a prodigious extent. As the boy begins to grow up, I shall show him quite impatient for his getting on, and urging his masters to set him great tasks, and the like. But the natural affection of the boy will turn towards his despised sister; and I propose showing her learning all sorts of things, of her own application and determination, to assist him in his lessons: and helping him always. When the boy is about ten years old (in the fourth number), he will be taken ill, and will die; and when he is ill, and when he is dying, I mean to make him turn always for refuge to the sister still, and keep the stern affection of the father at a distance. So Mr Dombey – for all his greatness, and for all his devotion to the child – will find himself at arms' length from him even then; and will see that his love and confidence are all bestowed upon his sister, whom Mr Dombey has used – and so has the boy himself, too, for that matter – as a mere convenience and handle to him. The death of the boy is a death-blow, of course, to all his father's schemes and cherished hopes; and 'Dombey and Son', as Miss Tox will say at the end of the number, 'is a Daughter after all'.

He went on at greater length, and the full text (or all that survives) can be read in Forster's biography. Dickens explained that he meant the daughter's love for her father to grow; and 'so I mean to carry the story on, through all the branches, and off-shoots . . . that come up; and through the decay and downfall of the house, and the bankruptcy of Dombey . . . when his only staff and treasure, and his unknown Good Genius always, will be this rejected daughter, who will come out better than any son at last, and whose love for him, when discovered . . . will be his bitterest reproach'.

There were still many uncertainties, of course. Dickens was not sure, for example, what to make of Walter Gay – a promising young fellow who enters the firm – and wondered if he could 'show him gradually and naturally trailing away . . . into negligence, idleness . . . and ruin'. Nor had he even yet thought of Dombey's second marriage, his contempt for his wife, and her flight from him across France with his manager, James Carker. But though much was left to work out, the way was clear.

He had, however, come to find writing difficult. He had expected to go slowly at first, but he continued to find writing an effort. It was not 'invention' that held him back (he even had to restrain himself from launching into extravagances) 'but the difficulty of going at what I call a rapid pace is prodigious'. It was the more serious because he had meant to write a new Christmas book as well as start *Dombey*, and as the months drew on he found it impossible. Nine years before, he had been able to keep two novels going at once, but he was more ambitious now, yet no longer so confident. He confided in one of his friends at Lausanne that he did not much care for *Pickwick*, just as a few years later he sadly wrote, 'the world would not take a Pickwick from me now'. He had a reputation to lose, and though pleased with *Dombey*, neither he nor his critics were in the least satisfied with his latest Christmas book *The Battle of Life*.

Having gone to Paris, as he had intended, he got on better. At Lausanne he had missed the 'magic lantern' of London, the life and variety of its streets at night, which he felt revived his imagination. Before leaving Switzerland for France he had learnt of the success of the first number of *Dombey*, and now he was able to do as planned, and write the death of Paul; at last, early in January 1847, he was able to tell Miss Coutts: 'Between ourselves – Paul is dead. He died on Friday night about 10 o'clock, and as I had no hope of getting to sleep afterwards, I went out, and walked about Paris until breakfast time next morning.'

When the number was published it made a strong impression. Today, the pathos seems so forced that we fail to notice that there was something new about it. In the number-plan Dickens had noted: 'Paul's illness only expressed in the child's own feelings. News of Paul's illness. No. Not otherwise described.' It was hardly too *sentimental*: an objection made at the time was that it was rather over-calculated – and certainly the repetition, from the end of the first chapter, of the image of dying as setting out on a 'dark and unknown sea', was carefully planned.

Lord Jeffrey, who had been so overcome by the *Old Curiosity Shop*, was unprepared. He had written enthusiastically to Dickens after the third number, saying, 'I am quite in the dark as to what you mean to make of Paul, but shall .watch his development'. Two months later he wrote: 'Oh, my dear, dear Dickens! What a No. 5 you have given us! I have so cried and sobbed over it last night, and again this morning. . . . Since the divine Nelly was found dead on her humble couch, beneath the snow and ivy, there has been nothing like the actual dying of that sweet Paul.' Thackeray was carried away. He threw the new number down, explaining, 'There's no writing against such power as this – one has no chance!'

There was a difficulty, however, and one that Jeffrey pointed out: 'After reading this climax in the fifth number, what are you to do with the fifteen that are to follow?' Dickens was aware of the problem, and made an emphatic note in his plan: 'Great point of the No. to throw the interest of Paul *at once on Florence*'. A few chapters later there are 'New Faces', and we are introduced to Mrs Skewton and her daughter Edith, the future second Mrs Dombey.

A new impetus was now given to the tale; and in spite of delays arising from the birth of Dickens's fifth son (and seventh child), he turned to the novel again with his old enthusiasm, writing to Macready of 'sitting in my smallest of temporary dens, with *one half of the current number yet to write* – with my thoughts so shaken by yesterday, that I cannot fall to work – and yet with such an infinite relish for the story I am mining at, that I don't care twopence for being behindhand, and hope to make a dash, a plunge and a finish, with what the people who entice you to play on the racecourses call, "A firm heart and a bold resolution, them as don't play can't win, and luck attend the Royal Sportsman!".'

Edith and her mother were new figures to set off against Florence; and as her brother had helped bring out her glowing love and affection, so her new stepmother's degradation was to contast with her innocence. Before he began to write about them, Dickens jotted down a sketch of the new characters in his notes: 'The mother and daughter. The mother, and her cant about "heart", and nature – Daughter who has been put through her paces, before countless marrying men, like a horse for sale – Proud and weary of her degradation, but going on, for it's too late now, to try to turn back.' Dombey marries her from pride, because of her rank and beauty that can be bought, and because she may provide another son. He tries to humiliate her, but she runs away with Carker his manager, whom she hates, and humiliates both husband and lover. For a second time all Dombey's hopes are destroyed, the House of Dombey is crushed, and only then are father and daughter united.

The effect is strange. The novel undoubtedly tries to re-examine the conventional novelistic view of women, but cannot reframe it in anything but a variation on the old stereotypes. Dickens knows not to accept them, but he is hardly able to think in fresh terms, can only see from outside, and is too well aware of the fact that his public was not ready to admit that there were difficulties. Edith may resent being 'put through her paces', but this is still how Dickens treats her. She is 'beautiful and stately', 'dumb and motionless', to the end. It is curious how Dickens, himself, even worked out the story in advance on the assumption that the way out of her marriage was to be by means of adultery: a situation he was quick to realise would have been impossible (for many reasons). Dickens allows us to see exactly what she is doing in refusing to accept her insufferable husband, but at the end, she is left alone with her 'devilish sorry' Cousin Feenix, and Dombey is allowed to revert to decent behaviour and domestic acceptability.

The whole subject is impossible, including the sub-plot about her step-cousin, Alice Marwood, and her mournful conversion. To permit us to feel a limited sympathy for these outcasts they are deliberately conventionalised. It was not just a situation that arose from Dickens's peculiar assumptions, widely shared as they were by his readers. Even several years later, the French critic Taine found to his surprise that Englishmen among themselves always spoke of adultery as a crime. The complications in the story are bizarre and absurd: acceptable only because we can see that the novelist has elaborated them to deal with situations he knows to be intolerable and under the stress of change.

He does wish to express his admiration for women, perhaps always implicit in his work with whatever reservations: 'Dombey and Son is a Daughter after all.' Polly Toodle is introduced as 'a good plain sample of a nature that is ever in the mass, better, truer, higher, nobler, quicker to feel, and much more constant to retain, all tenderness and pity, self-denial and devotion than the nature of men'. Toots exhibits Susan Nipper to us as an 'extraordinary woman'. Women play the more active part in the story, from the kitchen chorus up through Mrs Chick and Miss Tox, to Edith's high-flown dramatics. They play the predominant role to the end. Even Mrs MacStinger 'comes over' Captain Bunsby! Susan produces another daughter, 'a female stranger . . . and I'm glad of it'; and finally, instead of a reminder of Paul's death that Dickens once intended, there is an account of Dombey's devotion to his granddaughter, for 'no one, except Florence, knows the measure' of his 'affection for the girl'. The whole novel, is an indictment of all buttoned-up, patriarchal, masculine, 'manly' values.

'Dickens and women' has properly become a special topic, to be seen developing in the novels; but, as it happens, it has been dealt with most authoritatively through his biography. Rightly enough, feminist criticism has made us see much that had been formerly often ignored. But we also have to understand Dickens's response in the light of his own times. His own attitudes were often evasive, even opportunist, and a mixture of perceptiveness and compromise. So were those of his readers. The situation was changing, but the uncompromising feminist was seen as a figure of fun; the sensible woman was resourceful, adaptive, and ready to use her superior insight to turn the situation to her advantage.

The second main subject in the novel is the attack on the importance attached to money. Dombey uses money to cut himself off from all human feelings except a pride in his son. He tells Polly Toodle, when he engages her as nurse, 'When you go away from here, you will have concluded what is a mere matter of bargain and sale, hiring and letting'. He loses one wife with the thought that there is 'something gone . . . well worth the having', and invests in another; he looks on his riches as everything, until they have gone and he remembers Paul's question, 'Papa! what's money . . . I mean, what's money after all?'

To some extent it is just the old Dickensian moral that no one can be any good who is interested in money for its own sake; it is partly the teaching that the rich man cannot enter heaven; and it is also partly what Edmund Wilson calls Dickens's growing 'indictment against a specific society: the self-important and moralizing middle-class who had been making such rapid progress in England and coming down like a damper on the bright fires of English life'. When helping with negotiations for the financial backing of the *Daily News*, Dickens had come into contact with successful businessmen and company promoters for the first time; and John Chapman, said to be the 'original' of Dombey, had introduced him to the fraudulent 'Railway King' George Hudson (1800-71) – rather to Dickens's disapproval. It was a world he disliked and despised.

There has been an attempt to link Dickens's disapproval of such developments with his supposed regret for the past, and to trace both in his descriptions. He has been said to show the railway 'only as destructive', with no suggestion of hope or social progress. But this is quite wrong. It is an agent of change, like 'the first shock of a great earthquake', as in the marvellous description in Chapter 6; but though Carker is killed by an express, his end is deserved. To Toodle, as a stoker, it is something familiar after which to name his eldest child, 'Biler'. To Dickens, about this time, a railway journey was always 'wonderfully suggestive' and it was when travelling by train that he had the idea for his 'A Child's Dream of a Star'. Although the railway journey in Chapter 20 seems a symbol of death to Dombey, this is only at a time when he feels that everything he meets is 'setting up a claim to his dead boy'. Death is in his mind, not ours. For when the railway forces itself in through the wretched suburbs of the town, and Dombey looks out through the carriage window, 'it is never in his thoughts that the monster who has brought him there' has merely 'let the light of day in on these things: not made or caused them'.

Even so, the firm of Dombey and Son disappoints if we expect the novel to show what it was like to be a merchant-prince of the mid-nineteenth century; and although everyone who reads Dickens must agree by now that a childhood memory of his novels is useless for a mature understanding of his genius, the book is not just 'suitable for children', but much of its sentiment is curiously childish. Much is made of fairy-tale associations, and these are rather overworked. Again, it is one thing to have the setting for Florence's home vividly fancied from the child's point of view when she is left its lonely mistress (Chapter 23): the mansion in which 'dust accumulated, nobody knew whence nor how', where 'spiders, moths and grubs were heard of every day', and 'an exploratory blackbeetle now and then was found immovable upon the stairs, or in an upper room, as wondering how he got there'. It is quite another thing when this shades into a labouring appeal to feel with her 'true young heart' whatever is 'solemn . . . dim . . . murmuring . . . faint . . . far-off . . . soothing . . . wild, weak, childish . . . half-formed' or 'cruel'. It would be wrong not to discriminate between different levels and kinds in Dickens's writing, even though there is nothing to be gained from dwelling on the novel's weaknesses which are a certain childishness, a fairy-tale whimsicality, the obvious absurdities of Edith's pride, and the way in which the writer's skill is abused whenever he turns aside from life to a false drama which he has half-confused with the world of the stage and his own Christmas books.

No doubt largely because of the sentiment of Dombey and daughter it is an easy book to pillory; yet it can also be seen as marked by a 'bold, rapid and highly simplifying art'. It was the novel chosen by the English critic F. R. Leavis (1895-1978) to show that the poetic power he found in *Hard Times* could be discerned throughout Dickens's work. In *Dombey* Leavis saw proof of a 'poetic conception of his art' and an 'inexhaustibly wonderful poetic life' in Dickens's prose. Everywhere, he says, 'in description, narrative and dramatic presentation and speech, we have exemplified that vitality of language which invites us to enforce from Dickens the truth of the proposition that in the Victorian age the poetic strength of the English language goes into the novel, and that the great novelists are the successors of Shakespeare'. Dickens has his own tradition, we may say, which came not only through the English novel and the dramatists of the seventeenth and eighteenth centuries, but more directly through the impress of the language and imagination of Shakespeare – his sanity and the abundance of his characters – both on Dickens himself and on the culture of his readers.

It was exceptional for Dickens to traffic with critics. But, after finishing *Dombey*, he wrote to the editor of the *Sun* to ask him to give his 'warmest acknowledgements and thanks' to the writer who had reviewed the last number. He followed this with a short note to the reviewer – who turned out to be the editor, Charles Kent (1823-1902) – in which he said that 'he had never addressed a similar communication to anybody except on one occasion'. Yet, if we turn back to the *Sun* to see what moved him, it seems little more than a conventional though warmly enthusiastic tribute. Most of it is praise for the novel's 'many strange, original, life-like, and admirable characters. . . . For it is not the least important or the least remarkable among the numerous peculiarities of Mr. Dickens as a novelist . . . that he imparts to a fictitious being an absolute and visible individuality. The actors in his tales are . . . as actual as flesh and blood, as true as humanity'. It also recognises the vividness of occasional scenes, instancing the auction at Dombey's house (Chapter 59). It is clear that Dickens was still delighted at recognition of the lively actuality of his characters and the personal contact they seemed to give his readers with their author. 'An old friend has left us, the voice of a dear favourite is silent': this is the way in which Kent wrote of him and which Dickens welcomed; and this is at least partly how he hoped to be read. Dickens's authoritative command over his readers does largely depend on his 'voice': a poetic power over words which allows him to conjure into life the world and people of his imagination.

The conclusion of *Dombey* also brought him a letter from his old father-in-law, George Hogarth, whose review of *Sketches by Boz* had once pleased him so much. Dickens replied to say that he was 'quite as sensitive to applause' which he knew to be sincere, as he had been a dozen years before. He affirmed 'a great faith in Dombey, and a strong belief that it will be remembered and read years hence', and invited Hogarth to the *Dombey* dinner.

Such exchanges may remind us of something in the novels that is as clear in their origins as in Dickens's eventual public readings, as apparent in their genesis as in their fictional celebrations of fellowship in their eating and drinking, in the lustrous bottle of old Madeira, or in Captain Cuttle's extraordinarily delicate cooking for Florence (Chapter 49): that though of course they are linguistic structures, they are designed to awake and share feelings and sympathies.

Chapter 8

David Copperfield

IN APRIL 1848 Dickens began to organise another amateur production of Jonson's *Every Man in His Humour*, to raise money for James Sheridan Knowles (1784-1862), the dramatist, in order to establish him as curator of Shakespeare's house at Stratford. Dickens had already engaged in actor-managing several times before, and between 1847 and 1857 his amateur company appeared over thirty times in the provinces and about as often in London. He was obsessed with the theatre. Ostensibly the object was always a good cause; yet he had a portable theatre built in his new home, Tavistock House (where he moved in 1851), and to the last he was interested in drama for its own sake.

It was not just that he enjoyed acting. He liked managing quite as much, revelled in directing others, seeing to every detail of arduous tours and rehearsing each play with professional thoroughness. He could not relax without something to do. He often seemed to want to escape both from home life and from the imaginative world of fiction into one made up of endless details of little significance. It was because acting and managing made no demands on his creative resources, that he was able to expend such vast energy on them and remain fresher than anyone else at the end. He treated them like his charitable work for Miss Coutts, as a wilderness of practical demands into which he could retire in refuge from more pressing responsibilities. Just before he died he asked a friend what he thought one of his 'most cherished day dreams' was and gave the answer himself: 'To settle down for the remainder of my life within easy distance of a great theatre, in the *direction* of which I should hold supreme authority.'

Another activity which now took up a great deal of his time, was a reformatory home for 'fallen women' which he started for Miss Coutts. The idea of the home was to take off the streets women who sincerely wished to escape from such a life, clean up their manners and morals, and ship them off to the colonies. From 1847 to 1858, Dickens managed an administrative committee of the home, and undertook its supervision.

He was obviously interested in the psychology of the women he dealt with, but it is equally clear that he enjoyed nothing so much as practical decisions, from what was to be done about the drains to the problem of a girl found early in the morning with a policeman in the front parlour.

Yet even allowing for the fact that all his letters about the home were written to a Victorian maiden lady, they are unrevealing. In real life, Dickens had none of the sympathy for 'fallen women' that he showed in his books, or that men such as Wilkie Collins revelled in. With the exception of what he wrote about Little Emily and Martha in *David Copperfield*, he made little use of what he learnt there, and even Emily was untypical of the women in the home. One of his cardinal principles in encouraging the women to reform was that they should be allowed to look forward to marriage after they had emigrated; but at the end of *Copperfield* Dickens was careful to leave Emily a wilting spinster: 'A slight figure . . . kiender worn; soft sorrowful, blue eyes; a delicate face; a pritty head, leaning a little down. . . . That's Em'ly'.

He was still eager to set up a new weekly magazine. Even before the *Daily News* interlude, he had had similar ambitions and, by the summer of 1849, he wrote: 'I think I have, without a doubt, *got* the Periodical notion.'

In planning it he relied on Forster for practical advice; and they decided on a weekly miscellany, made up of stories and articles 'in the liveliest form' they 'could be given'. Above all it should appeal to the imagination: but by method of treatment rather than choice of subject. It was to sell for twopence, be printed by Bradbury & Evans, with W. H. Wills (1810-80), a practised journalist, as assistant editor, and Dickens as proprietor, and to come out as *Household Words* in March 1850.

No-one was better than Dickens at starting a magazine, this time on the right lines and under his firm control. New contributors were recruited, such as Mrs Elizabeth Gaskell (1810-65), who had come to the fore with her novel *Mary Barton*. Dickens wrote to her that there was 'no living English writer' he would 'desire to enlist in preference'. To Mary Howitt he explained that he was 'particularly anxious to deal with . . . all social evils, and all home affections'; and, in 'A Preliminary Word', he declared that the new work was 'to bring into innumerable homes, from the stirring world about us, the knowledge of many social wonders, good and evil'.

The first two volumes of *Household Words*, especially, were used to preach social reform, largely in matters of public health. The imitator of Addison devoted much of his time to articles about London's sewage system, then of great topical interest. *Household Words*, in fact, is extremely unlike the sort of magazine Dickens had once had in mind, to be called *The Cricket* or *The Robin*. Even W. H. Wills, who was efficient but dull, vainly appealed to his chief for something comic; and it was only when Dickens felt 'an uneasy sense of . . . a want of something tender' in the second number that he bestirred himself to write 'A Child's Dream of a Star'. Yet the event showed that he had judged the public correctly. After only a fortnight, he could write to Miss Coutts: 'Household Words . . . will become a good property. It is exceedingly well liked, and "goes", in the trade phrase, admirably. It was hard work to start, but to establish it firmly would be to gain such a great point for the future (I mean my future) that I think nothing of that.'

Meanwhile, he had begun *David Copperfield*. He had started thinking of it late in 1848 and had then decided on a holiday before he began. Accordingly, he had set off with some friends to Norwich, to explore the scene of a recent multiple murder, and then on to Great Yarmouth by coach. Dickens was delighted with the way in which 'the town and tide' were 'mixed up like toast and water'; and, although he had not yet thought of a plot for the new book, he was determined to work into it a description of his latest discovery. His visit 'was the success of the trip'. Yarmouth 'is the strangest place in the world . . . I shall certainly try my hand at it'. At first he did not know how. In February he began seeking a title. He was evidently thinking deeply about the new book, so that his mind 'was running like a high sea'. He started writing just in time for publication on 1 May. Though the novel is remarkable for showing a further advance in the way it was planned, Dickens never had more than one number in hand once serialisation began. He even overheard someone in a shop ask for the next number before a word of it had been written, which gave him 'a vivid sense of mingled enjoyment and dismay'.

He began with difficulty: 'My hand is out. . . . Though I know what I want to do, I am lumbering on like a stage waggon, and . . . the long Copperfieldian perspective looks snowy and thick'. Yet he did what was needed. In the first number, three of the novel's main themes are provided for, and we are introduced to the Peggottys, the Murdstones and Betsey Trotwood, who do not merely represent three sets of characters to be developed according to the author's whim, but whose part in the perspective is already sketched out.

It was with the second number that he had a remarkable idea. For the past two years he had had by him the autobiography of his childhood. At his wife's suggestion it had been given up. But now that he was writing in the first person for the first time, he saw a great opportunity. Into the second number went the account of his own childhood reading; into the third went memories of Wellington House Academy; into the fourth were inserted, almost unaltered, the story of the blacking-factory (changed to Murdstone & Grinby) and his desolate life in London. 'I really think I have done it ingeniously,' he wrote, 'and with a very complicated interweaving of truth and fiction.' Micawber appeared in the same number; and throughout the novel the seeds of his recollections blossomed in the most out-of-the-way corners and crevices and in a way detectable even to some of his readers at the time.

Copperfield has a special place: just as it stands in a central position in the succession of his novels, with seven before and seven after, so it unites the ease of writing of his youth with his growing sense of design. For the twenty-part novel, with sixty or more chapters, an autobiographical narrative had several advantages. It developed naturally by several stages, and, as the story stretched over a longer period, it was less crowded and easier to follow. Dickens had grasped that characters might be shown as they develop; and, although still tentatively, David, Uriah and Dora do develop, while others at least seem to do so.

We have sometimes been bedevilled by E. M. Forster's thinking about 'flat' and 'round' characters. In Leavis's plaintive words, 'all the girls' school English mistresses in England seized on the distinction' – quite fairly. Yet analysis was not what Dickens was after. He wanted to show characters as vividly as possible in speech and appearance. If he praised other novelists, it was in terms of their force, originality and skill in expression. Like Trollope he held that it was the novelist's business to present his characters as 'speaking, moving, human creatures'. They both would have rejected Henry James's dictum that 'a character is interesting as it comes out, and by the process and duration of that emergence'. The remark is untrue and can never be true of comedy.

Dickens's method has now to find a theme, plan characters and setting, and only lastly a plot to unite them. This was one reason why he was always in agonies of thought for months before he started. Forster, with whom it had been discussed, even held that in *Copperfield* 'more than in any other of Dickens's novels . . . the incidents rise easily and to the very end connect themselves naturally and unobtrusively with the characters of which they are a part', because there is a main theme running through it: 'a unity of drift or purpose . . . apparent always. . . . We learn the value of self-denial and patience, quiet endurance of unavoidable ills, strenuous efforts against ills remediable; and everything in the fortunes of the actors warns us, to strengthen our generous emotions and to guard the purities of the home'. So varied are the characters and humour, and so artfully meandering the course of events, that what Forster said about the purpose used to be overlooked. It now seems obvious that the novel has a central theme. It is partly suggested in the great chapter 'Tempest', with David's opening words: 'I now approach an event in my life, so indelible, so awful, so bound by an infinite variety of ties to all that has preceded it in these pages, that, from the beginning of my narrative I have seen it growing larger and larger as I advanced . . . and

PLATE 5:   Emily, by Browne, from the title page of *David Copperfield*.

throwing its forecast shadow even on the incidents of my childish days.'

Much was foreshadowed as early as Chapter 3, in a passage Dickens added in proof when his draft of the first number was complete. How much of it was actually planned in advance can be judged only after a careful comparison of Dickens's part-plans with a close reading of the book, and what it cost him to write can be seen in a letter to Forster: 'I have been tremendously at work these two days . . . with the Ham and Steerforth chapter, which has completely knocked me over.' Two days later he wrote that he was 'in a tremendous paroxysm', and that the chapter was still 'on the Anvil'. Emily's fall is foreseen when she tells David she wants to be a lady and runs out along a baulk of timber overhanging the water. Steerforth's death is foreshadowed, and Ham's implicit in Emily's fears for her uncle and Ham when out at sea: 'I wake when it blows . . . and believe I hear 'em crying out for help. That's why I should like so much to be a lady.' The chapter about the tempest ends with an old fisherman approaching David:

> He led me to the shore. And on that part of it where she and I had looked for shells, two children – on that part of it where some lighter fragments of the old boat . . . had been scattered by the wind – among the ruins of the home he had wronged, I saw him lying with his head upon his arm, as I had often seen him lie at school.

It was as he had seen him on the first night at Salem House, and again when he stayed with Steerforth for the first and last time and, looking into his room when he was about to leave, found him 'fast asleep . . . with his head upon his arm, as I had often seen him lie at school'.

Emily's story runs as an identifiable strand through *Copperfield*; and David, Steerforth and Emily are all children who have grown up without a father. It was Mrs Steerforth's boast that her son had never been denied anything, and David himself says that as he grew up he found that he too had 'an undisciplined heart', which had to learn that there are times when it must subdue itself to others.

To Forster, everything shows that a true marriage and loyalty to the 'purities of the home' are the underlying subject. It is brought out strongly in the story of David, Dora and Agnes, and is the only good reason for the flabby story of the Strongs and Maldons; it links Steerforth with Emily, and even the lesser characters, such as Aunt Betsey and her mysterious husband, Peggotty and Barkis, the Traddleses and the Micawbers. When Betsey Trotwood calls David's mother 'a very Baby', in Chapter 1, and she confesses that she 'was but a childish widow, and would be a childish mother if she lived', Dickens already had David's child-wife, Dora, in mind.

It is a pity that the story of Dr Strong and his wife, and the suspected seducer, Jack Maldon, was felt to be needed to underline this theme. Dickens's heart does not seem to be in it, and it is almost pointless until it comes to a climax in Chapter 45 when Annie Strong explains that though she had married so young she is proud of her husband. For '*there can be no disparity in marriage like unsuitability of mind and purpose*'. Annie goes on, 'If I were to be thankful to my husband for no more, I should be thankful to him for having saved me from the first mistaken impulse of my undisciplined heart'.

It is easy to see why David finds these words so impressive. He repeats them as he leaves the Strongs, and the chapter ends with a fanciful symbol recalling the state of his own marriage to Dora, 'Little Blossom': 'My mind was still running on some of the expressions used.

. . . "The first mistaken impulse of an undisciplined heart". . . . But we were at home; and the autumn winds were blowing.' In the next chapter about Dora, when David makes a last attempt to 'form her mind', 'these words . . . were constantly recurring to me . . . for I knew now that my own heart was undisciplined when it first loved Dora'.

Every character has a place in the design, and this was so new for Dickens that one of his friends reviewing the first number in *The Athenaeum*, even thought that Aunt Betsey had been drawn 'in pure waste', and that she had vanished for good at the end of Chapter 1. But those days were over. Far from casually introducing a character that would come to nothing, Dickens commited the fault of resuscitating some when their parts were finished. Murdstone re-appears preparing to marry another heiress; and Littimer and Heep in jail are another device to fill out a novel of unwieldy length.

Improvising was over. A crisis, for example, arose when a neighbour of Dickens discovered that he had taken her as the 'original' of his portrait of the volatile dwarf, Miss Mowcher. She could see how Miss Mowcher, as Steerforth's friend, was to be made a procuress for Emily, and was deeply hurt at having her deformity held up to ridicule. She wrote Dickens a despairing appeal; but far from being remorsefully anxious to make amends, he rather unwillingly agreed to change the development, and explained that it would take him several months. In time he did all she wished, but only at the cost of painfully changing his intentions.

Miss Mowcher, however the reader views her, remains one of Dickens's greatest comic characters. The richness and variety of the comedy in *Copperfield* ought not to be taken for granted. The serious nature of the design was something more or less new in Dickens's work, and it is so much easier to go about analysing the plot and structure than to appreciate the comedy. But Micawber and Miss Mowcher do more than leave a mere 'impression' that they have sometimes had too much attention. They start up to life before our eyes and deserve our wonder.

We have been too quick to see Dickens's characters as conventional or stereotyped. Certainly some are; others are modifications of convention. Dora, Steerforth and David himself are not simple stereotypes; or at the very least they offer variations on the expected. What are we to make of 'Daisy' David's weakly romantic adoration of his friend, or of Steerforth himself? Other figures are unique conceptions, even one with as verbally limited and modest a part as Barkis, with a death-scene that outdoes Falstaff's. 'Conventional' is the last word to apply to Dickens.

Dickens succeeds with his comic characters because they live in their dialogue. Even Mrs Micawber seems vividly alive because she is of the same stamp as Mrs Nickleby and Mrs Gamp. They all live in their speech. Every natural turn of phrase is caught up, turned and arranged in a glorious succession of sparkling inanities and wit, nonsense and telling shrewdness, and phrases that we at once recognise as our native speech transformed into dialogue past man's 'tongue to conceive or his heart to report'. The definition of a 'round' character is that it is capable of giving us 'a happy surprise'. yet there is no need to confine this to psychological development. Characters such as Mrs Micawber and her husband, Miss Mowcher and Mrs Crupp are capable of giving 'a happy surprise' every time they open their mouths.

The purely comic characters are supported by comic grotesques and others who are only gently humorous or odd. Mr Creakle introduces himself, 'I'll tell you what I am . . . I'm a Tartar', Uriah recounts his loathsome family history: 'Father got the monitor medal by being umble. So did I. . . . "Be umble Uriah", says father to me, "and you'll get on."' Mr Murdstone begins a problem of arithmetic, 'if I go into a cheesemonger's shop and buy five thousand double Gloucester cheeses at fourpence-halfpenny each, present payment . . . '. Yet the oddities of many of the characters are subdued. They are shown as people David knew, and depicted as he might have remembered them. It is another advantage of the autobiographical narrative that it sometimes restrains Dickens's natural exuberance.

The weakest parts are the serious characters, such as Ham, Emily and the Strongs. They strike the right attitudes but have nothing to say. Dora cannot be dismissed so easily: Dickens had the advantage of writing about a real situation, not only in the sense that it was close to his personal experience but one of universal possibility. 'That there are certain faults in the book,' as John Forster says, 'is certain', yet none 'incompatible with the most masterly qualities.'

As the central novel of Dickens's development, and as fictionally and actually autobiographical, *David Copperfield* was particularly close to the author. He was clear about this when he wrote in the preface, 'I do not find it easy to get sufficiently far away from this Book' and that 'no one can ever believe in this Narrative, in the reading, more than I have believed it in the writing'.

Published about the same time as William Wordsworth's (1770-1850) *Prelude* it is a great English autobiography. So much of its power lies in the way it is told, as the 'narrative' of 'my written memory'. As he writes of the storm when Steerforth is drowned:

I dream of it sometimes. . . . I have an association between it and a stormy wind, or the lightest mention of a sea-shore, as strong as any of which my mind is conscious. As plainly as I behold what happened, I will try to write it down. I do not recall it, but see it done, for it happens again before me.

The novel is about those who are part of David himself in memory, such as Dora and his mother – 'Can I say of her face . . . perished as I know it is – that it is gone, when here it comes before me . . . as distinct as any face I may choose to look on?' He is aware of how much his sense of self depends on a memory aroused by associations of words, places, people, events and physical associations:

> I don't know why one slight set of impressions should be more particularly associated with a place than another, but I never hear the name, or read the name, of Yarmouth, but I am reminded of a certain Sunday morning on the beach, the bells ringing for church, little Em'ly leaning on my shoulder, Ham lazily dropping stones into the water, and the sun, away at sea, just breaking through the heavy mist, and showing us the ships, like their own shadows.

David is undefeated by his secretly unhappy life. Even when dividing his time between Murdstone & Grinby's and the prison, he enlivens the Orfling with his fancies as they watch the rising sun gilding the Thames, and makes stories for himself 'out of the streets and out of men and women'. And even as his thoughts go back 'to that slow agony' of his childhood, he writes with pride, 'When I tread the old ground, I do not wonder that I seem to see and pity, going on before me, an innocent romantic boy, making his imaginative world out of strange experiences'. The long Copperfieldian perspective leads to fulfilment. As David and Agnes learn of each other's love and thank God, 'long miles of road' open out before his mind, and he recognises 'toiling on . . . a ragged way-worn boy forsaken and neglected, who should come to call even the heart now beating against mine, his own'.

We are brought at last to see Agnes as standing for more than herself, a symbol of how love can lead to fulfilment and higher purpose. For, as they are at last united, 'clasped in my embrace,' David writes, 'I held the source of every worthy aspiration I had ever had; the centre of myself, the circle of my life, my own, my wife; my love of whom was founded on a rock'. As Hillis Miller explained*:

> David's relation to Agnes is a late example of that transposition of religious language into the realm of romantic love which began with the poems of courtly love, and which finds its most elaborate Victorian expression in *Wuthering Heights*. David has that relation to Agnes which a devout Christian has to God, the creator of his selfhood, without whom he would be nothing.

Already, if sketchily, Dickens thought of his (and David's) 'unhappy

---

*J. Hillis Miller, *Charles Dickens, The World of His Novels*, Harvard University Press, Cambridge, Mass., 1957.

want of something' in life, as more than a lost love, and expressed it partly as a need for the 'religious dimension'.

Reviews written at the time are disappointing, too concerned with the book's moral teaching. Yet Thackeray generously asked, 'Who can rival this great genius?' The novel has never lost its popularity, and won Dickens as many new readers as Pickwick, among them some who had felt too fastidious to enjoy anyone so popular. Years later the poet and critic Matthew Arnold (1822-88) wrote:

> There is a book familiar to us all . . . I mean *David Copperfield*. . . . What a pleasure to have the opportunity of praising a work so sound, a work so rich in merit. . . . To contemporary work so good . . . we are in danger perhaps of not paying respect enough, of reading it (for who could help reading it!) too hastily. . . . What treasures of gaiety, invention, life are in that book. What alertness and resource! What a soul of good nature and kindness governing the whole!

Chapter 9

Bleak House and *Hard Times*

EARLY IN 1851 Dickens began dramatic activities for the Guild of Literature and Art, preparing his company for a royal performance. In March John Dickens fell seriously ill and died. Catherine Dickens was unwell, in the care of doctors at Malvern. Then, while Dickens was speaking for a public charity, news was brought of the death of his youngest daughter, Dora. Forster had to tell him, after a speech in praise of his friend's 'practical philanthropy' as a writer, during which someone called out 'Humbug!'

Dickens continued his amateur acting, moved to an even larger house in Tavistock Square, and was 'wild to begin a new book'. By 7 December he wrote 'I have only the last short chapter to complete No. 1', and in March 1852 *Bleak House* was published. Sales surpassed all expectations, and when the novel was finished he could write, 'it beat dear old Copperfield by a round ten thousand or more. I have never had so many readers'.

It begins as an autobiographical novel about a young woman teacher, Esther Summerson, who is rather like Jane Eyre. But, to enlarge its scope, the narration alternates between Esther – who uses the past tense – and the conventional third person who uses the present.

Esther's own story is straightforward melodrama; yet the novel shows a variation in structure in the way it is made to open out like a painted fan until we see the whole of contemporary society from the Dedlocks' mansion to the denizens of the London rookeries. And everything radiates from, and converges on, the Court of Chancery, where the interminable case of Jarndyce *v.* Jarndyce has been proceeding for the past forty years.

The language is closer in texture, more allusive, more fanciful and sometimes almost metaphysical. 'I have purposely dwelt on the romantic side of familiar things', wrote Dickens in his preface; and, though this was said as an afterthought at the end of a defence of the possibility of Spontaneous Combustion, it is a welcome sign that he had come to see that he was never meant to be a complete realist. Though, like other novelists of his time, Dickens never published any considerations of his art, he knew well enough what he was doing.

When someone criticised him for overloading his narrative with imaginative fancies, he wrote to Forster:

It does not seem to me to be enough to say of any description that it is the exact truth. The exact truth must be there; but the merit or art in the narrator, is the manner of stating the truth. As to which thing in literature, it always seems to me that there is a world to be done. And in these times, when the tendency is to be frightfully literal and catalogue-like . . . I have an idea (really founded on a love of what I profess), that the very holding of a popular literature through a kind of popular dark age, may depend on such a fanciful treatment.

When Bulwer Lytton made the same sort of criticism, Dickens was prepared to admit that he sometimes so delighted in an unusual idea that he might 'pet it as if it were a spoilt child', adding that he did not deny or question the charge, 'otherwise than upon this ground – that I work slowly and with great care, and never give way to invention recklessly, but constantly restrain it; and that I think it is my infirmity to fancy or perceive relations in things which are not apparent generally'. It was G. H. Lewes who attacked Dickens for the absurdity of Krook's spontaneous combustion, and it was the novelist George Eliot (1819-80) who followed Lewes's precepts in a long dissertation in *Adam Bede* in which she attacked novelists who cannot 'write the exact truth'. After Dickens's death, Lewes went further, and criticised him along the same lines in an article in the *Fortnightly Review* answered by Forster. Yet it was the allegedly less intellectual Dickens who grasped that novels depend on playing on the difference between what is real and imagined, and that if they give 'the exact truth' they cease to be fiction.

It is too simple with this novel to say (as Forster did) that 'the characters multiply as the tale advances, but in each the drift is the same', and perhaps this is why he felt driven to admit that it 'suffered by the very completeness with which the Chancery moral is worked out'. Yet it is true that everyone is somehow connected with the case of Jarndyce *v*. Jarndyce, and that the whole book is a unified study of society. The Court of Chancery is not only representative of corruption and social decay, but is itself symbolised by the junk-shop kept by Krook, known as the 'Lord Chancellor', and his savage cat expressive of 'strict statutes and most biting laws'. His tenant, poor mad Miss Flite, has her place in the scheme, and his own death symbolises the end 'of all authorities in all places under all names soever, where false pretences are made and where injustice is done'.

In this, and in the comic relish with which he exposes political corruption at Chesney Wold, lies part of Dickens's greatness as a satirist. Whatever the 'Chancery moral' is, it ought to include Sir

Leicester Dedlock's conversations with his cousin Volumnia about the general election, and his horror that his housekeeper's son (a successful industrialist) has been invited to go into Parliament, or Lord Boodle's after-dinner conversation with Sir Leicester:

> 'Supposing the present Government to be overthrown, the limited choice of the Crown, in the formation of the new Ministry, would lie between Lord Doodle and Sir Thomas Coodle. . . . Then, giving the Home Department and the Leadership of the House to Joodle, and the Exchequer to Koodle, the Colonies to Loodle, and the Foreign Office to Moodle, what are you to do with Noodle? . . . What follows? That the country is shipwrecked, lost and gone to pieces . . . because you can't provide for Noodle!'

This is good fun but should not be taken too seriously. It should be clear that such satire is never the 'exact truth', and that it was an oblique comment on the real world of Victorian government. So we should not follow George Bernard Shaw (1856-1950), who praises it for its '*accuracy*', but enjoy it as a burlesque. What truth there is lies in its understanding of the relations between classes; in the way it shows a breakdown even within the Dedlocks' marriage, and still more between Sir Leicester and the people he claims to represent; in the representation of the 'iron barrier' (Chapter 8) between the life of the brickmakers and those like Mrs Pardiggle who bring them tracts they cannot read; in the break-up of several of the families; and the way in which everything that is 'natural' gives way to what has been devised as a matter of system.

For much of the art of the novel and the pleasure it gives lie on the surface: in the dialogue, the manipulation of the characters, and in the assured and flexible tones of the writer whose triumph in presenting his novels (and himself through his novels) was of course quite as much one of art as of character. It is true that, to his public and to himself, his personality and his work were always closely related, and that by the majority of his readers they have often been seen as one and confused. It was even a natural result of the way he wrote and his idea of himself as an entertainer that it should result in a cult of his personality. Yet none of this was inconsistent with his highest achievements and with his giving a wonderfully controlled and brilliantly sustained performance. To ask for a novel by Dickens without the sense of his presence would be to ask for something *less*. This apparent presence of the writer is not just in the scenes directly taken from life as in *Copperfield*, in the fictional autobiographies of Esther Summerson and Pip, or in the occasional passages in which the novelist seems to speak out directly, but in almost every turn of phrase, every conception, and in the world he creates. For, as a novelist, Dickens is always what he once planned to be if he could speak to his readers through his own periodical, 'a sort of previously unthought of Power', and 'inseparable companion', always present in his work, and to be found not only in obviously forceful passages, but in the vitality of his language and the sense it gives of someone continuously presenting his scenes.

We can instance the opening chapter, almost all those which are set in Chancery and Cook's Court, the eloquence of Skimpole, or the smooth surface of Tulkinghorn which inspires Dickens to writing about him instead of simply presenting what he says. With these are the passages in the novel which show melodrama at its highest. Chapter 48, 'Closing in', for example, presents a marvellous succession of scenes, from Lincolnshire to London, from the world of fashion and the dismal grandeur of the Dedlocks' town mansion, to the departure of Tulkinghorn through 'the wilderness of London', to his chambers in Lincoln's Inn Fields. For:

> In these fields of Mr. Tulkinghorn's inhabiting, where the shepherds play on Chancery pipes that have no stop, and keep their sheep in the fold by hook and by crook until they have shorn them exceeding close, every noise is merged, this moonlight night, into a distant ringing hum, as if the city were a vast glass, vibrating.
> What's that? Who fired a gun or pistol? Where was it? . . .

All such scenes show Dickens's verbal resourcefulness. They may shade into staginess, bathos and near dullness when the serious characters have to carry the story forward, yet even the flattest scenes have the resource of purpose and precision.

At the same time, to argue that much of the art is on the surface is not necessarily to be blind to what Edmund Wilson calls 'the symbolism of more complicated reference'. This symbolism goes beyond what we have already seen, the way in which Krook expressly 'symbolises' the Lord Chancellor; his shop, the system of law; his tenants, its victims; his death, the consequences. The symbols here each stand for something; they are no more nor less than what the nineteenth-century novelists often spoke of as 'allegory'. Throughout everything Dickens writes he shows that this was one of his most constant modes of thought; and however complex the correspondences may be, there is still usually a clearly discernible framework of meaning: Chancery stands for the whole of England, or all authorities whatsoever; it corresponds to muddle and confusion between classes, in government, in social conditions, and then in religion and in the human condition itself. Much of this is obvious; for whenever the victims of Chancery die, for example, Nemo, Jo, Gridley, Richard, Tulkinghorn and Lady Dedlock, the wider implications are stated or implied. We are turned, from time to time, in other directions than the criticism of society; Jo on the street corner, looking up at the great cross of St Paul's, may possibly be thinking 'that sacred emblem to be . . . the crowning confusion of the great confused city'; and there is Miss Flite with her caged birds, 'Hope, Joy, Youth, Peace, Rest, Life, Dust, Ashes, Waste, Want, Ruin, Despair, Madness, Death, Cunning, Folly, Words, Wigs, Rags, Sheepskin, Plunder, Precedent, Jargon, Gammon, and Spinach!' And besides this, there is the way in which the novel stands for the whole world of Dickens's imagination, his way of looking at life, including its ambiguities and contradictory elements, his uniquely personal feelings; and to come at this one must accept that the novel also stands by and for itself.

Yet it can never stand entirely by and for itself. Addressed to its own times, it cannot escape its context which is part of its language. Attempts to see the novels as autonomous lead to the difficulty that in opening interpretation to almost all possibilities, many of these are lost. It takes the patience and scrupulousness of Hillis Miller, in his chapter on *Bleak House*, to show the 'special quality of Dickens's imagination', and how he seeks to 'get behind the surface by describing all of it bit by bit'. For the novels are so extraordinarily full of possibilities and meanings, and these all lie within such dense and imaginative verbally realised life, that to broaden the range of inter-pretation can be self-defeating. Anyone can seize on a train of images or themes, and trace them through the novel. But to go further and re-arrange themes or patterns foreign to Dickens's purpose or against the grain of his culture, misses his intense wish to engage with the actualities round him and make his readers do the same. The life in the novels is so abundant that, denied the reader's attention to narrative and the sense of an author urgently addressing the reader – their first and fundamental principles – they even tend to diffusion and chaos.

In itself, the value of finding new themes is limited. It is too easy. Very simply, one might take as a single theme, for example, 'the need for Love': one which is centred on Esther, branching out in her relations with her 'darling' Ada, with the deprived Jellyby children, with everyone at Greenleaf, Miss Flite, the brickmakers' women, the Coavinses, and – obviously – with Jarndyce and Allan Woodcourt. There is clear textual justification for linking whole groups of satellite characters with the same theme. Underpinning the whole plot structure and motivating its events, moreover, is the love of Esther's mother and Captain Hawdon which is still so strong after his death, that (as Edmund Wilson says) it pulls the world of the novel apart. In a real sense this *is* a major theme, and we could easily find more.

Such dissection may lead to seeing less than the whole. Such themes do not simply help to offer something for everyone; they are effectively made part of each other in the story to unite in an overwhelming impression of life; and to achieve nothing less than to give such a total impression, apparently all-embracing, expressed with personal intensity, and told as a story, was the challenge Dickens now met and overcame with each of his novels.

There is a constant pull in opposite directions for anyone trying to account for Dickens. We may try to explain *what* he is saying, or *how* he is saying it, and it is often right to insist that his language is almost everything. Yet not quite. Each approach, taken by itself, is evasive. Mere delight in, or discussion of, instances of imagery and syntax, the sound and structure of his phrases, subtlety of tenses, and everything that can be recognised and named after the close reading of a chosen passage, has the advantage of directing attention to what Dickens wrote and not rewriting it in another form. But that, too, may be a retreat from an intimate response to the novel. Then, what the *Quarterly Review* once said of *Vanity Fair* is true of several other mid-Victorian novels with the same linguistic density:

> It is impossible to quote . . . with any justice. . . . The whole growth of the narrative is so matted and interwoven together with tendril-like links and bindings, that there is no detaching a flower with sufficient length of stalk to exhibit it with advantage.

Yet detach them we should and trace the relationships, provided we recognise the impossibility of summing up so complex an 800-page novel in a few hundred words.

It is a work that raises many questions. The student is made to ask what has happened to the way the story is told: the alternate chapters of the ironic, present-tense impersonal narrator, and the apparently artless, hardly reflective past-tense narrative by Esther. He might consider the artificiality of the whole convention: whatever conjuring trick has shuffled the two packs so neatly together and set them into the conventional form of a monthly serial? What is gained? – Then, what has happened to Esther? She seems to be conceived as someone whose sensitivity to her illegitimacy and her treatment in childhood has been over-compensated for by her resolve to be dutiful and good; but after such an excellent initial conception, Dickens has lost his nerve in dealing with an actual woman, and spoilt his experiment. If Dickens's conceptions are often blunted when elaborated, are there not teasing implications in many of the relatively minor characters, such as Inspector Bucket, Rouncewell or Miss Flite? To George Orwell (1903-50), in a marvellous phrase, the novels are 'rotten architecture, but wonderful gargoyles' – but, in another sense, is not the whole much greater than the parts? Do they not in fact, fit together, if in a very Gothic fashion, to make a total impression?

Once again, one of the chief characters is drawn from someone Dickens knew personally: Leigh Hunt, who is shown as the brilliant but selfish Harold Skimpole. What impelled Dickens to do it? Whatever the explanation or excuse it is clear that the resemblance was extraordinary and immediately recognisable. Dickens altered Skimpole's Christian name (at first Leonard), changed him from thin to fat, and told his illustrator to make him 'unlike the great original', but the likeness remained! Dickens boasted of it. Even after he had been warned against it, he broke out in a letter: 'I suppose that he is the most exact portrait that was every painted in words! . . . I don't think it could possibly be more like himself. . . . There is not an atom of exaggeration or suppression. It is an absolute reproduction of the man.'

That is exaggerated, too. Yet what *was* like was the way they both spoke, too close even to be called parody. Once seen, the direct allusion has a pointed meaning. Hunt was despised by Dickens as a lapsed radical, a 'lost leader', someone half dishonest, who had betrayed the calling of professional authorship and abased himself before the Whig aristocracy. The characterisation widens out into showing a betrayal of the whole alliance between art and liberalism. It stands even without recognition of the personal allusion, but sharper with it, and it may remind us that though photographic realism is not Dickens's aim he did mean to reveal an essential truth. This applies to the use he makes of the whole scene of London: St Paul's cross, the doorway of the Society for the Propagation of the Bible in Foreign Parts, the iron gate to Nemo's graveyard (from boyhood memory) and every part of the legal quarter. The reader should feel it as a familiar scene which vouches for Dickens's vision.

The book was finished in September 1853, after which he made a short tour of Switzerland and Italy with Wilkie Collins and another friend. Earlier in the year he, and other members of the Guild, attended a banquet to Literature and Art at Birmingham, where he spoke about the place of Literature, explaining that he gloried in writing for a wider public than writers of the past, and that the People had set writers free 'from the shame of the purchased dedication' and 'from the scurrilous and dirty work of Grub Street'. Literature, in return, could not 'be too faithful to the People' in the 'cause of their advancement'.

While at the banquet he heard of a plan to start a new literary and scientific centre – the Birmingham and Midland Institute. At once he made an offer to give a public reading of *A Christmas Carol* in support: 'There would be some novelty in the thing as I have never done it in public, though I have in private, and (if I may say so) with great effect on the hearers.' His offer was eagerly accepted, and three readings were duly given in Birmingham Town Hall immediately after Christmas. They were a success. The audience was extremely responsive and, after a moment's doubt about 'whether he could conceal the requisite effort', they were soon at ease and 'all going on together . . . as if we were sitting round the fire'. When he came to the moment when the Ghost of Christmas Present introduces Scrooge to the two children, he read with emphasis. 'This passage,' a reporter says, 'was magnificently given, and brought down a burst of applause that clearly indicated in what direction the sympathy of the audience lay.' Such incidents help to show the connection between the response to Dickens's works and contemporary life. The previous week the same hall had been used for a conference on reformatory schools, and the *Birmingham Mercury* commented that Dickens had won 'the admiration and affection of a large proportion of the British people', because they saw in him 'a household teacher – a fireside expositor of the great educational and social questions about which the legislature is AT LAST beginning to trouble itself'.

Among the new subjects to which Dickens now turned was the question of relations between Capital and Labour. In Italy, his attention had been caught by reports of the Preston weavers' strike; so, at the end of January, when it was in its twenty-fourth week, he visited the town. He was thinking of writing an article about it for *Household Words*, and already had a new novel in mind which might deal with life in the industrial north. As a writer he was disappointed with Preston; but, as someone who sympathised with the workers, he was greatly impressed with the orderly way in which they managed the strike. He refused to admit that either side was entirely right, and his published conclusions have a modern ring in demanding 'authorized mediation': for, 'masters right, or men right, . . . there is certain ruin to both in the continuous or frequent revival of this breach'.

The novel was started in January 1854 and finished in July at Boulogne. It had been called for largely because the circulation of *Household Words* had fallen and it was felt that only a serial by Dickens could pull it round. On publication, in April, sales doubled in the first ten weeks and went on climbing; and it was another triumph which Dickens felt was crowned by its dedication to Carlyle.

Hard Times is short, compressed, powerful, mannered, more or less consistent, easily discussable and not entirely typical of Dickens. F.R. Leavis's criticism has also focused attention on it. He argued that it was a 'moral fable', or fiction with a clear purpose, and that Dickens's writing showed 'a full critical vision, a stamina, a flexibility combined with consistency, and a depth that he seems to have had little credit for'.

As Leavis says, Dickens's main intention was 'to comment on

certain key characteristics of Victorian civilization'. Dickens was concerned about the difference between Fact and Fancy, and emphasised with all his power that this was not just a rhetorical antithesis: that mere fact, or logic, which leaves half of our lives out of account – any way of controlling conduct or affairs, that lacks sympathy, love, and understanding between human beings – is not merely sterile but bitterly destructive of all the moral virtues, beauty, and everything that is best; that a sound life cannot exist without happiness; and that the proper education of children must take into account their moral development, to be fostered through their imagination and love of life. The government of a country cannot just be administered from self-interest, nor trusted to a single class. The relations between Capital and Labour (or 'Masters and Men') can never be properly managed if it is assumed that they must be in a perpetual conflict, or the men inevitably subject to the paternal rule of the masters. Above all, the relations between men and women, between father and children, mother and child, or brother and sister, between friends, or any persons in almost any permanent association, must originate and be rooted in liking, affection or love.

The novel was thus a protest not only against certain characteristics of *Victorian* society, but against tendencies to be found in any industrial civilisation: a protest against all repression of the human spirit by the letter of the classroom, the constitution, the law, and the so-called principles of political economy. Dickens's purpose was not just to strike at everyday, run-of-the-mill, mid-nineteenth-century 'utilitarianism' – and especially not at anything so abstract as the Utilitarian philosophy as expounded by Jeremy Bentham (1748-1832) and J.S. Mill – but to aim at all kinds of social abuses which he thought ran counter to human life and happiness because they were framed according to supposed 'facts' while they ignored obvious human needs. That is why even the circus ring was better than the cinders of Coketown or the dust and ashes of the political arena. The novel has a broad purpose even though it includes references to some of Dickens's living contemporaries which most of them were unable to recognise, and satire of specific abuses which was too pointed to be understood by the general reader; and it is only by understanding this broader purpose that one can see how it unifies Dickens's remarks on Stephen Blackpool's marriage, the aesthetic theories of the 'third gentleman' (Chapter 2), the problems of Trade Unionism, Louisa's marriage, and her brother's theft from the Bank. Dickens said that the ideas in the book took him 'by the throat' and forced him to write. A careful reading shows that he succeeded in giving them a unified purpose.

As a study of industrial relations, it is still highly debatable. There is no way of disputing that in Stephen Blackpool we have another experiment in characterisation that has gone wrong. He may have been conceived as a markedly flawed character, but the current of the story carries him off into passive martyrdom. Slackbridge is close enough to a type of rabble-rousing trade-unionist but he is not representative – any more than Bounderby. The reason for Stephen's refusal to join in the strike is foolish and soon forgotten. There is no doubt that some of the argument is interwoven with the wish to show that mere utilitarian rationalism is an unsatisfactory guide, whether in deciding to allow one's repulsive wife to poison herself (Book 1, Chapter 13) or (for Harthouse) to seduce the wife of a constituent. But of the novel as a whole the reader must be asked 'to make the best' of it 'and not the worst'.

In other ways Dickens's view of industrial relations was by no means simple-minded. He was not alone in his dilemma. He is clear about the right to strike, but thinks it almost always wrong to use it. He disliked rigid employers and disruptive trade-unionists; he was in favour of all attempts at conciliation; and wanted the Government to set up an independent body to arbitrate. Speaking to working-men at this time he spoke happily of the value of education in bringing together 'employers and employed', and 'in the better understanding of those whose interests are identical'.

He was neither an apologist for industrial capitalism, nor a fundamental critic. Still less should we conclude that he was even a minor prophet in the line of Ruskin and William Morris (1834-96) as social critics. In spite of the praise Ruskin deservedly gave the novel for its teaching on general education and political economy in *Unto This Last*, its other implications would have disturbed him deeply. And though Shaw wrote, in an important introductory essay, that 'Dickens's occasional indignation' had 'spread and deepened into a passionate revolt against the whole industrial order' (Waverley Dickens, 1912), this is wrong if we take it to mean that Dickens protested against the arrival of the machine. For there are other unperceived topicalities (mainly in Chapter 2) which show that he meant to satirise recent enlightened attempts to improve industrial design in his own worst Bounderby manner; and although he dropped this satirical intention as he went on, it is a clue to a tendency within the novel. Dickens is essentially varied and paradoxical. Ruskin also summed him up acutely, in writing immediately after his death: 'Dickens was a pure modernist – a leader of the steam-whistle party *par excellence*. . . . His hero is essentially the ironmaster.'

Too much can be made of the industrial scenes in the novel, in comparison with the domestic life of the Gradgrinds and the circus, though Dickens himself was responsible for calling attention to them when he began to write. He chose as part of his subject a dispute in the cotton industry just when the Preston strike was in everyone's mind. He wrote an article on Preston for *Household Words* just before the first instalment of the novel; and then, even before *Hard Times* had finished its serial run, he advertised as its successor Mrs Gaskell's *North and South* (1854) which was also partly based on the Preston dispute. The book is typical of Dickens in that it is essentially general and curiously topical. Part of a complete understanding of Dickens is to appreciate how he wrote for the readers of his time. Yet the further this is pursued, the clearer it is that he used topicality as a means of *communicating* – it never becomes his true subject. This goes even further than he could explain, as he once tried to do in a letter to an American publisher about this time:

> I think it possible that I have considered the powers and purposes of fiction a little longer and a little more anxiously and attentively than your lady friend. To interest and affect the general mind in behalf of anything that is clearly wrong – to stimulate and rouse the public soul to a compassionate or indignant feeling that it *must not be* – without obtruding any pet theory of cause or cure, and so throwing off allies as they spring up – I believe to be one of Fiction's highest uses. And this is the use to which I try to turn it.

In effect, however, he aroused the public through fiction, and used public issues both to awaken his creative force and to hold his readers' attention. (Not unreasonably, he did not care to make precise distinctions.) It was a circular approach. He used events men knew about in order to speak to them more directly, and then tried to write the truth about their relations with each other. For certainly *Hard Times for These Times* should be interpreted as a moral fable, even as a 'morality' drama based on Christian morality.

When Sissy, the adopted circus-girl, chats with Louisa, the clever daughter of the 'practical' Mr Gradgrind, she reports her slow progress at school and tells how 'after eight weeks of induction into Political Economy, she had only yesterday been set right by a prattler three feet high, for returning to the question, "What is the first principle of this science?" the absurd answer, "To do unto others as they would do unto me" '.

Or she tells Louisa how the schoolmaster had set her some problems saying that

> 'in a given time a hundred thousand persons went to sea on long voyages, and only five hundred of them were drowned or burnt to death. What is the percentage? And I said, Miss,' here Sissy fairly sobbed, . . . 'I said that it was nothing.'
> 'Nothing, Sissy?'

'Nothing, Miss – to the relations and friends of the people who were killed. I shall never learn.'

In many ways the story is to be read less as a fable than a parable. If not read thus, Stephen's fall down Old Hell Shaft, at the end, and the star he thinks he can see as he lies dying, would be a tasteless piece of sham piety:

'I ha' fell into a pit that ha' been wi' th' Fire-damp crueller than battle. I ha' read on't in the public petition . . . fro' the men that works in pits, in which they ha' pray'n an pray'n the lawmakers for Christ's sake not to let their work be murder to 'em. . . . But look up yonder, Rachael! Look aboove!'

Following his eyes, she saw that he was gazing at a star.

'It ha' shined upon me,' he said reverently, 'in my pain and trouble down below. . . . Often as I coom to myseln and found it shinin on me down there in my trouble, I thowt it were the star as guided to Our Saviour's home. . . .

They lifted him up, and he was overjoyed to find that they were about to take him in the direction whither the star seemed to him to lead. . . .

They carried him very gently along the fields, and down the lanes. . . . It was soon a funeral procession. The star had shown him where to find the God of the poor; and through humility, and sorrow, and forgiveness, he had gone to his Redeemer's rest.

Of course Dickens was attacking society, but not – as Shaw asserted – to arouse revolution, but in the name of Christian charity.

It is time to mention Dickens's religion, so difficult to pin down. Biographically speaking, he seems to have been brought up partly as a nonconformist, to have been a unitarian for a time in the early 1840s, and to have become an intermittent churchgoer towards the end of his life. He felt a need for religion, but little for worship, and hated dogma. Theologically speaking, it might be said of him, as Shaftesbury said of his brother-in-law, the whig statesman Lord Palmerston (1784-1865), that he did not 'know the difference between Sydney Smith and Moses'. It may be true that he could 'never be properly described as a religious man', but as Orwell admits, 'he "*believed*" undoubtedly'. Orwell refers to a letter Dickens wrote in 1868 to his youngest son:

You will remember that you have never at home been harassed about religious observances, or mere formalities. I have always been anxious not to weary my children . . . before they are old enough to form opinions respecting them. You will therefore understand the better that I now most solemnly impress upon you the truth and beauty of the Christian Religion, as it came from Christ Himself, and the impossibility of your going far wrong if you humbly but heartily respect it. . . . Never abandon the wholesome practice of saying your own private prayers, night and morning. I have never abandoned it myself, and I know the comfort of it.

Dickens wrote prayers and a *Life of Our Lord* for his children which were pious and sincere. William Ewart Gladstone (1809-98), the future Liberal prime minister, rather ludicrously remarked of *Nicholas Nickelby* that there was 'No church in the book, and the motives are not those of religion'; and another critic of the day wrote of Dickens as 'the prophet of an age which loves benevolence without religion' (*Rambler*, 1854). But it is a mistake to suppose that any church has a religious monopoly; and it is on religious feeling that Dickens founds his plea for benevolence.

He was sometimes unsure, but he would not have written the same books without a religious faith. His guide was the parable of the Good Samaritan. Unsatisfactory as that may be – to some – his belief was expressed not simply at the level of his readers but at that of the majority of humanity.

Again, although as early as the 1850s the part of an Englishman's nature which 'found gratification in religious life' was often already 'drifting into political life' (as Beatrice Webb found) both these approaches were still often interpreted in terms of each other. This was not just habit, but because Christian values were still widely enough accepted to stand against those of material success. The contrast between them is at the heart of Dickens's novels. Whether he was declaiming about 'the duties of a Christian government', as in his address 'To Working Men' (1854), or asking his children (as in his Will) 'to try to guide themselves by the teaching of the New Testament', his writing is convincing; and it is so not because its power came from the simple faith of his readers but because of his own broad conviction.

Chapter 10

Little Dorrit and society

DICKENS WAS SPENDING more of his time in France, though it was not the gaiety of Paris that attracted him but its life and air of efficiency. He admired the French talent for getting things done; and, after visiting an important exhibition, felt how even English painters lacked 'character and purpose' in comparison, and that there was 'a horrid respectability about the best of them . . . strangely expressive . . . of the state of England'. Personally he disliked Napoleon III and his anti-liberalism, but the more he thought about politics the less faith he had in the future of parliamentary government in England.

Unfortunately he thought about politics increasingly, and as he grew impatient for reforms convinced himself that Parliament was a failure. His problem was that he could find no alternative, yet he seemed untroubled by this inability. When war was declared on Russia in 1854 he rightly saw that it would be used as a further pretext for putting off necessary social reform, and once it was clear how disastrously the army had fared in the Crimea, he was convinced that the government was both incompetent and corrupt.

In fact he had little faith in it from his days as a parliamentary reporter. Early in 1854 he wrote that 'it does so little and talks so much that the most interesting ceremony I know of in conjunction with it was performed . . . by one man [Cromwell], who just cleared it out, locked up the place, and put the keys in his pocket'. Eighteen months later he wrote to Forster, 'I really am serious in thinking . . . that representative government is become altogether a failure with us'; and, soon after, to another friend, 'As to the suffrage, I have lost hope even in the ballot'.

Generally speaking, Dickens avoided direct political pronouncements; but, less than a year before his death, he provoked a storm of disapproval when he summed up his creed in a speech at Birmingham: 'My faith in the people governing is infinitesimal; my faith in the People governed, is, on the whole, illimitable.' He had to explain by stressing that politicians made up the first set of 'people'; but he could never explain how the 'People' themselves were to find an acceptable government. To the *Times* this seemed like 'the sentiments' of someone from 'St. Petersburg or Pekin', who 'would not be likely to get a hearing there'. Dickens was a brilliant entertainer, an admirable moralist and an effective social critic, but not a serious politician.

Perhaps he was right, therefore, to interest himself in a new movement at the time which was simply in favour of Administrative Reform. He made one of his most brilliant speeches at a meeting in 1855. 'He was gravely in earnest,' it was reported, 'when he denounced the Prime Minister for his heartlessness and flippancy in the face of disaster.' 'The first great strong necessity,' Dickens wrote after the meeting, is 'to carry the war dead into the Tent of such a creature as this Lord Palmerston, and ring it into his soul . . . that Dandy insolence is gone for ever.' A month later he started *Little Dorrit*.

The new work was his greatest social satire, certainly one of his darker novels, with many unattractive characters, a complicated plot and less enlivening humour.

He had been happy with autobiographical narrative in *David Copperfield* and *Bleak House*, and now that he returned to a tale in the third person he relapsed into all the old intricacies he had used as long ago as *Oliver Twist*. He even seemed distrustful of his new skill; for though in William Dorrit, the Father of the Marshalsea, he was able to make the narrative grow partly out of character, Rigaud, Flintwich, and Tattycoram are mainly dummies from the Dickens waxworks. Each has a dark secret, and near the end of the story all grew so involved that, for the first time, Dickens felt it necessary to write a 'Memo for working the story round', to see how the characters were connected and what problems were left to be solved.

Much of what is best in Dickens still remains. Many of the characters are as full of life as ever. The inhabitants of Bleeding Heart Yard have a new credibility. Cavaletto is amusing, Pancks in the old style, Casby cleverly done, and his daughter Flora marvellously memorable. She was Dickens's admired Maria Beadnell, who, remembering her young lover as she read about David Copperfield's courtship, had written to remind him of the old days. She was married now, she said, and 'toothless, fat, old and ugly'. Dickens was enraptured at the thought of meeting her, and shocked when he did. 'Dora Spenlow' had become 'Flora Finching':

> Flora, always tall, had grown to be very broad too, and short of breath; but that was not much. Flora, whom he had left a lily, had become a peony; but that was not much. Flora, who had seemed enchanting in all she said and thought, was diffuse and silly. That was much. Flora, who had been spoiled and artless long ago, was determined to be spoiled and artless now. That was a fatal blow.

Like his hero, Arthur Clennam's, Dickens's eyes 'no sooner fell upon the subject of his old passion, than it shivered and broke to pieces'; and *Little Dorrit* is the work of a man disillusioned by everything he turns to.

A main strand in the narrative is the story of Little Dorrit herself, the young heroine who had been brought up in a debtors' prison, and who never ceases to love her old humbug of a father. She is only slightly portrayed, and as a fictional character is tiresome in her lack of reality. The central figure is William Dorrit, who has been in prison so long that he is known not only as her father, but as the Father of the Marshalsea. Like Mr Micawber he was partly based on memories of John Dickens as he had been when shut up in the same prison walls. He is vain, pompous, and above all patronising. He represents everything that exasperated Dickens in his smug, self-satisfied fellow-countrymen, who were content to be imprisoned within old ways by their government, or shut up in a set of their own stupid conventions, as long as they could preserve an appearance of genteel respectability. According to Gissing, 'the subtlest bit of humour in all Dickens's books' is the scene in which Dorrit entertains an old pensioner from the workhouse, Mr Nandy. It certainly combines all Dickens's expert observation and mastery of dialogue with his new wry disillusion; and though we may regret the loss of his old optimism, his new outlook gave him a fresh view and a further insight into character.

Linked to the Dorrits are the Clennams. Mrs Clennam represents all that is fierce and hard in repressive religion. She has shut herself up in an old house brooding over old wrongs. Arthur Clennam, her son, eventually marries Little Dorrit. Through Arthur there is a link with the Meagleses, with whose daughter Pet he had been in love before he encountered Little Dorrit. The Meagles family is linked with a Miss Wade, who tells her own story within the novel, 'The History of a Self Tormentor'. Pet marries a dilettante artist, Henry Gowan, type of all that Dickens detested in members of his own profession, insincere and incapable of taking anything seriously. The Gowans are linked with the Barnacle civil servants and the money-making Merdles; and the Merdles intermarry with the Dorrits. The crucial thing about the novel is not that Dickens was not altogether successful with the plot, but that he discovered how to manipulate a vast range of characters, and to bring them into relation with one another so as to reveal how the greater part of society was a sham.

This was something new: too new for him to sacrifice the machinery of plot completely. But it is clear that he had half a mind to do something of the kind when he began. 'It struck me that it would be a new thing,' he wrote, 'to show people coming together, in a chance way, as fellow-travellers, and being in the same place, ignorant of one another, as happens in life; and to connect them afterwards, and to make the waiting for that connection a part of the interest.' He was unable to do this, but was obviously not really interested in the mere intrigue, and much more concerned to impose a single atmosphere on the book and give it unity of mood. This is done partly by consistency of style, partly by a succession of inter-relating images. The collapse of Mrs Clennam's house, the crash of the financial 'house' of Merdle, and the ruin of the rather obviously contrived symbol of William Dorrit's 'castle in the air' were all part of a plan. The imprisonment of Dorrit in the Marshalsea, of society within the bonds of convention, of enterprise under state inefficiency, of those in quarantine at the start of the book, and those in the prison at Marseilles, all also have their place in a scheme. Dickens planned it; and as fast as the story opened out, he kept it together. 'Society, the Circumlocution Office and Mr Gowan,' he wrote to Forster 'are of course three parts of one idea and design.' It is not the most entertaining of Dickens's novels; Thackeray called it 'damned stupid'; but if only for the principle of its design *Little Dorrit* deserves, with *Bleak House*, a special place in the history of the novel.

The book had another purpose and a startling effect. It was an attack on financial corruption and political incompetence in English society. Chapter 10, 'Containing the Whole Science of Government', and Chapter 21, in which the swindling financier Merdle gives a grand dinner-party for the Barnacles, are among the best things he wrote. Mr Merdle is more than the share-pushing cheats of *Nickleby* and *Chuzzlewit*: he is congratulated by a representative from the Treasury, on being 'one of England's world-famed capitalists and merchant-princes'. Yet his exposure remains much less than an attack on nineteenth-century capitalism, and it is doubtful how far it was meant to be anything of the kind. He would be a fraud under any system.

In fact no one objected to the exposure of Merdle. No one could. What some readers did resent was the attack on the Civil Service and government in the description of the Circumlocution Office. As a satire, this is beyond praise: 'The Circumlocution Office was (as everybody knows without being told) the most important Department under Government. No public business of any kind could possibly be done at any time, without the acquiescence of the Circumlocution Office. Its finger was in the largest public pie, and in the smallest private tart.'

Dickens poured all his contempt for officialdom into the description of Lord Tite Barnacle and his vast family who had all fastened themselves to the national ship. How they ran their departments according to the sublime principle of 'How Not To Do It', is skilfully linked with a description of how the same principle was practised by those actually in the Government. 'Public Departments and professional politicians' are mentioned together. The Circumlocution Office is said to have been 'a nursery of statesmen', the Barnacles of the hustings. As a satiric exposure of some of the realities of government at that particular time it was completely justified. But whether it is right to regard it now as a satisfactory and complete analysis of mid-Victorian society would be quite another matter.

That some biographers have simply accepted and praised the 'truth' of its social insight is clear. The exception was Orwell, who saw that Dickens fantastically simplified what he was writing about:

> At the back of his mind there is usually a half-belief that the whole apparatus of government is unnecessary. Parliament is simply Lord Coodle and Sir Thomas Doodle, the Empire is simply Major Bagstock and his Indian servant, the Army is simply Colonel Chowser and Doctor Slammer, the public services are simply Bumble and the Circumlocution Office – and so on and so forth. What he does not see is that Coodle and Doodle . . . *are* performing a function which neither Pickwick or Boffin would ever bother about.

It is essential to read Orwell's essay. It should be realised, too, that Dickens fully believed that conditions were so bad that a revolution might break out in England at any moment. He wrote to Austen Henry Layard (1817-94), the leader of the administrative reform movement, that he believed that the discontent was 'extremely like the general mind of France before the breaking out of the first Revolution, and in danger of being turned by any one of a thousand accidents . . . into such a devil of a conflagration as never has been beheld since'. He continued to fear this, on and off, for the rest of his life. He was completely mistaken; and he was mistaken because his analysis of society was mistaken.

The counter-attacks made on him were usually inept. It was almost impossible to answer a work of fiction. One exception was a reply made by James Fitzjames Stephen (1829-94), the barrister and journalist, in the *Saturday Review*. Stephen was responsible for a series of slashing attacks on Dickens, and most of what he wrote can be dismissed. Even this attack can be discounted because of his personal reasons for defending the Civil Service. But the main point of Stephen's remarks was that he wanted to write not on behalf of the bureaucracy but of parliamentary government. 'Whatever else our Parliament is,' he wrote, 'it is the only popular government in the world which has been able to maintain itself . . . and there is no country in which the great ends of civil society . . . are more fully maintained or in which the private character of public men stands higher. . . . Our statesmen may sometimes provide for their cousins and nephews in the public service, but they do not sell their official secrets, or make fortunes on the Stock Exchange.'

This may be thought a fair reply, for though Dickens had also been shocked by the activities on the Bourse, France was his ideal. In a burst of irritation, he reduced Miss Coutts's companion, Mrs Brown, to tears when she once said something slighting about the French. It should also be remembered that Dickens never explained what he would put in place of the institutions he attacked. His limitations no doubt help to make him more effective as a satirist, but his own pretensions as a social prophet must not go unquestioned.

In fact, it is arguable that Dickens's political views were affected by his private troubles. His growing radicalism came not only from his observation of the changing state of the country but also from his own changing attitude to life. He was finding less pleasures in his success, for the greater it was the harder it grew to maintain. He seemed to know no rest except in action; and as Forster wrote:

> Not his genius only, but his whole nature, was too exclusively made up of sympathy for, and with, the real, in its most intense form, to be sufficiently provided against failure in the realities around him. There was for him no 'city of the mind' against outward ills, for inner consolation and shelter. It was in and from the actual he still stretched forward to find the freedoms and satisfactions of the ideal, and by his very attempts to escape the world he was driven back into the thick of it.

One of the mysteries of *Little Dorrit* remains its significance as Dickens's attempt to create a 'city of the mind' as a refuge from all that harassed him. If *Hard Times* represents, as it does, a somewhat superficial linking of Christian ethics with everyday life, then *Little Dorrit* and *Our Mutual Friend* show successive stages in an escape from everyday reality which was connected with his private life. How far this new extension of his fictional world is a success is also another matter altogether.

In *Little Dorrit* the religious dimension is perceptibly marked out. Although the English critic Humphry House (1908-55) remarked that 'religion had no part in the original conception' of Mrs Clennam, this is mistaken; her Old Testament ethic is contrasted with the New Testament spirit of Little Dorrit from the first. By the end, Little Dorrit is an allegorical representation of divine grace, as 'every morning' she ascends to Clennam's room in prison, 'winged to his heart bringing the heavenly lightness of a new love'. She is also the voice of Nature, and of the happier memories of childhood. As she and Mrs Clennam pass over London Bridge together, 'great shoots of light' stream 'among the early stars, like signs of the blessed later covenant of peace and hope that changed the crown of thorns into a glory'. And as the sun strikes on the black prison gate which had closed behind her when Clennam had turned her away, we are also told that its 'long bright rays' strike 'aslant across the city . . . bars of the prison of this lower world'. So there are two worlds, in one of which we are shut in, even by the bright rays of the sun.

Elsewhere, symbolic references are brought into play about the 'darker road of life' (Book 1, Chapter 26), and the ferry by which Clennam passes across the river on the way to see his earlier love, 'Pet' Meagles. It symbolises Time, and as Clennam gazes on the 'real landscape and its shadow in the water', he sees that 'there was no division; both were so untroubled and clear, and, while so fraught with solemn mystery of life and death, so hopefully reassuring to the gazer's soothed heart, because so tenderly and mercifully beautiful'. The two worlds are one.

Thus the symbolism of imprisonment is obviously one that goes beyond man's relation to society and involves the whole condition of life. Structurally, and in detail, it is finely worked out so that it greatly extends the novel's meaning; but the writing is so much less certain and pointed in parts clearly meant to be spiritually affirmative that this side to the novel is sometimes unsatisfying.

It is, nonetheless, written affirmatively, and introduces us to a new Dickens, and a different kind of man from the one he has often been thought: editor, actor, reformer, boon companion. His distress at this time, which precedes the breakdown of his marriage by several years, shows Dickens's own difficulty in coming to terms with himself. Clennam's position in the novel has been said to show 'an analogy to the familiar elements of a religious crisis', perhaps reflecting Dickens's own situation. With most men, indications of such a state of mind might have been expected to appear in the documents of his biography; but it can hardly be traced anywhere except in his letters to Forster, until the complete break that came with the collapse of his marriage. Stray clues can certainly be detected in the terse and rather unrevealing Book of 'Memoranda' which he began in January 1855, from which Forster printed extracts in his chapter, 'Hints for Books Written and Unwritten'. They include some of the key images of the novel, such as the ferry by the peaceful river. It has some entries that might be read as applying to Dickens himself, 'the man, always, as it were, playing hide and seek with the world, and never finding what Fortune seems to have hidden when he was born'. He writes of 'the man who is incapable of his own happiness. Or who is always in pursuit of happiness. Result, where is happiness to be found then. Surely not everywhere'. He was anxious to escape from preoccupation with himself, and writes with contempt of 'the man whose vista is always stopped up by the image of himself. . . . Would be a good thing for him if he could knock himself down'; and, though this note was later hastily marked 'Done in Podsnap' (of *Our Mutual Friend*) it applies to many characters in *Little Dorrit*.

Such is the tone of the early entries, when the 'motes' of *Little Dorrit* were 'floating in the dirty air', and they agree with the well-known but little emphasised letters Dickens had been writing to Forster at about this time. For, as early as *Copperfield*, Dickens had foreshadowed one of his memos in evidently thinking of himself (like David) as seeking 'realities in unrealities', and complaining of 'the old unhappy loss or want of something'. Then, later, but still as early as 1856, he suddenly wrote to Forster:

> Again I am beset by my former notions of a book whereof the *whole story* shall be on top of the Great St. Bernard. As I accept and reject ideas for *Little Dorrit*, it perpetually comes back to me. Two or three months hence, perhaps you'll find me living with the monks and Dogs a whole winter. . . . I have a *serious* idea that I shall do it, if I live.

Can he have been 'serious' about such 'a whole story'? He had proposed living in a Swiss monastery two years before, and he writes of himself in his letters as being driven in life by an 'irresistible might . . . until the journey is worked out', as if he were one of 'the restless travellers' of *Little Dorrit* on 'the pilgrimage of life'. Forster speaks of his trying to escape the world as an attempt to get 'the infinite' out of 'the finite'. In writing to another friend (Mrs Watson, 7 December 1857) Dickens says: 'Realities and unrealities are always comparing themselves before me, and I don't like Realities except when they are unattainable'. There is, from this time, a great division between the realities and unrealities of Dickens's life, though it is hard to trace, so closely did he keep it to himself.

We should understand that Dickens's biography cannot be told as a clear, uncluttered story. At this stage in his career, it is a second-best way of getting to know him. We must recognise that by now he was infinitely more subtle, reserved and conscious of playing a part than biographers have usually allowed.

His inner concern was sometimes apparent in spite of himself; for like his own characters he had found that the shadow of his past only lengthened the further he left it behind. As he moved up the social scale he showed some resentment at class divisions and a hidden lack of ease. He did not restrain his increasing impatience with administrative incompetence of various kinds. His disquiet may show in his retirement to France, and comes out in a letter from Paris in 1856: 'The old days – the old old days. Shall I ever, I wonder, get the frame of my mind back as it used to be then? . . . I find that the skeleton in my domestic closet is becoming a pretty big one.'

Chapter 11

Separation and
A Tale of Two Cities

DICKENS'S UNREST GREW, and the 'skeleton' became harder to conceal. Eventually, just a year after finishing *Little Dorrit*, he separated from his wife. When the crisis came it happened suddenly; but it was reached only after several years of unhappiness. Yet, though the main outline of events is fairly clear, the real feelings of those concerned and what drove Dickens and his wife apart are hard to explain.

Dickens himself was so extraordinary that it may be difficult to understand the power of the driving-force which took control of him at this time and allowed him neither rest nor relaxation. Even when he was writing a novel, editing, working for Miss Coutts, or indulging in amateur theatricals, he was often still so restless as to feel 'as if the scaling of all the Mountains in Switzerland . . . would be but a slight relief'. To tire himself enough to sleep, he took to walking, through the night, from Tavistock Square to a new house he had acquired at Gad's Hill, near Rochester. Anyone can offer to analyse him, but the stress under which he lived is hard to imagine.

Catherine Dickens had become a good, kind-hearted matron, with rather a reserved manner and fat little wrists over which her bracelets would sometimes come tumbling into the soup! As the years went by, she seems not surprisingly to have suffered from some kind of nervous illness, but no-one who knew her ever had anything to say of her but praise. Yet even that was always vague. Hans Andersen thought that she was exactly like Agnes Wickfield, and it may be that we sympathise with her or not according to our own temperament.

Dickens's dissatisfaction went back several years, but the immediate trouble came in 1857. In 1856 Wilkie Collins wrote a play called *The Frozen Deep*, which Dickens produced at Tavistock House in January 1857. His friends flocked to see it, and Thackeray declared that 'if the man would now go upon the stage, he would make his £20,000 a year'. The story is about an arctic explorer (Dickens's part) who saves his rival and dies in the arms of the woman he loves; and it was an exception to Dickens's usual parts in that it deeply stirred him. He derived 'a strange feeling' from it, 'like writing a book in company; a satisfaction of the most singular kind'. Six months later it was acted for charity by the amateur company, and professional actresses were

PLATE 6:   Ellen Ternan.

needed for some provincial performances; so Dickens engaged a well-known actress, Frances Ternan, and her daughters Ellen and Maria.

Dickens's letters are full of praise for the elder Maria, but his attention had been caught by the fair-haired eighteen-year old Ellen. It had been an old joke, when it had been merely an amateur company, for the 'Manager', as Dickens was called, to pretend to fall in love with his leading actresses; but he suddenly found the joke turning serious. It was just because he was so unaccustomed to such affairs that he was completely helpless: it seemed that nothing could be done about it.

He and Wilkie Collins went on holiday, and collaborated in a sketchy little series of articles called *The Lazy Tour of Two Idle Apprentices*, and *The Perils of Certain English Prisoners* for the Christmas number of *Household Words*. Dickens wrote to Collins:

> I want to escape from myself. For when I *do* start and stare myself seedily in the face, as happens to be the case at present, my blankness is inconceivable – indescribable – my misery amazing. . . . The domestic unhappiness remains so strong upon me that I can't write, and (waking) can't rest, one minute. I have never known a moment's peace or content, since the last night of *The Frozen Deep*. I do suppose that there never was a man so seized and rended by one spirit.

He confided to Forster (no mere Podsnap) who, though kind, was outspoken and drew attention to the other point of view. Dickens replied, writing about Catherine:

> God knows she would have been a thousand times happier if she had married another kind of man. . . . I am often cut to the heart by thinking what a pity it is, for her own sake, that I ever fell in her way. . . . There is plenty of fault on my side, I dare say, in a way of a thousand uncertainties, caprices and difficulties of disposition.

The result was almost inevitable. He cut himself off from her, and decided to busy himself with a series of paid public readings from his own works, starting on 29 April 1858.

There was a great row as the gossip broke out, partly through some of Dickens's in-laws, the Hogarths. As well as Ellen Ternan it involved Catherine's sister, Georgina, who had lived with the family since 1842 and who had stayed out of admiration for Dickens and to look after the home. She was wrongly suspected of being involved. We can skip the details of furious family disputes, legal wrangling, harmful publicity and frantic letters to friends. In the end, Catherine Dickens was dismissed with a good reference, much bad feeling on her husband's part, and an allowance of six hundred pounds a year.

Dickens would never back down, and to keep up appearances gave several major speeches in May and June. He also issued a public statement about the separation in a personal address in *Household Words*. It indirectly led to further resentment, and a wave of rumours which left Dickens with a 'sense of wrong' and the feeling, as he said, that his heart was 'jagged and rent out of shape'. For, in spite of much that has been written, there is little doubt that, for the time being, Dickens was as overtly innocent in his relations with Ellen Ternan as he said, though his air of outrage was hardly justified.

The justification for bothering with such an account is that it gives us insights into Dickens, uncertain as they may be. In the preface to his next novel he was actually to invite readers to relate his fiction to his own experience; and we have to keep this in mind, however ambiguous his comments and uncertain the rules of the game. Nor can we fail to be interested in it as an outburst from Dickens, already the member of an older generation, growing rather ill at ease with the changing status of women in the 1850s and 1860s both within marriage and more generally. We may also wish to try to analyse all that he tells us about his earlier relationships and his childhood and adolescence. Drastic conflicts were clearly set up within him: he claims pure innocence, responsibility and the freedom to do exactly as he likes in the same breath. Dickens's inclination towards such a freedom of feeling and attachment has already been seen in the novels as, for example, in David's love for Steerforth being said to be greater than ever directly after his friend has seduced Emily (Chapter 32), in the barely subdued admiration for Lady Dedlock, or the dubious legitimacy of Arthur Clennan. These are the desperate endeavours of a Victorian romantic to have everything both ways, simply shown in personal relations. The situation is familiar in the mid-nineteenth century elsewhere than in Dickens as well. We have to laugh at him when he seriously suggests to Forster that a good title for his next periodical might be *Household Harmony*. His controlled combination of passion and responsibility, excess and restraint, always in tension, has broken down.

He kept some friends and others fell away. Miss Coutts, for example, clearly sympathised with Catherine and was somewhat jealous of his interest in a younger woman; and he gave up any share in the work they had enjoyed. Amateur acting was over. For a time he did not want to write. The only solid work ahead came from a break with Bradbury & Evans, which meant ending *Household Words* and starting a new periodical, *All the Year Round*, the first number of which was to appear on 30 April 1859 with a new story by himself.

As usual it was hard to begin, but by March he was able to tell Forster: 'I have got exactly the name . . . A TALE OF TWO CITIES.' It was to be about the French Revolution; and, having enlisted the help of Carlyle, who lent him some books, he settled to work. Both the sale and the periodical in which it was published made a great impression with the first number, and by the fifth the circulation of *All the Year Round* was three times that of *Household Words*.

The novel was rather experimental as Dickens was still uneasy at writing in short weekly instalments. So he tried to make it almost completely narrative and worked closely over the story to see that it ran swiftly, unchecked by the need for appearing week by week. He had set himself, he said, the task of making it '*picturesque* . . . rising in every chapter with characters true to nature, but whom the story itself should express, more than they should express themselves by dialogue'.

It is easy to find improbabilities in the plot – forced into it by compression – but it has the design Dickens intended: rising from the dramatic scene on the Dover Road at the opening, and leading to the sensational climax, at which Carlyle declared 'it's wonderful' and Forster turned 'white with admiring approval'. Only Wilkie Collins hinted he could have done it better; and Dickens turned on him promptly with the fair retort that if it 'had been done in your manner . . . it would have been overdone'. The intention of the work was *not* to create a mystery or arouse suspense, but to reveal a developing pattern in the relations between the characters and a great historical event.

It has been remarked how curiously well its mid-Victorian author knew what it felt like to be caught up in revolution and to live in a police-state; and in its power to express this the novel is a masterpiece. We can see that this was partly learned from Carlyle's history of *The French Revolution*, as Dickens acknowledged. And its most insistent theme was the same as Carlyle's: that certain conditions must always lead to anarchy and anarchy destroys itself: 'There is not in France . . . a blade, a leaf, a root . . . which will grow to maturity under conditions more certain than those that have produced this horror. . . . Sow the same seed of license and oppression over again, and it will surely yield the same fruit according to its kind.'

Dickens, however, had a faith in the aims of revolution even stronger than Carlyle's though he had a hatred of how men might try to achieve them. It has been forgotten that he well knew what a police-state was from living in Italy. He was a close friend of such revolutionaries as Manin and Gallenga, who tutored his daughters. His true story of 'The Italian Prisoner' in the *Uncommercial Traveller* is extremely moving. He had lived through a period of revolutions in Switzerland, Italy and France, and it is this which helps to give a dynamism to his insight into the events of 1789. As it happens, the first number of the novel appeared on the very day that *The Times* reported revolution in Florence (30 April 1859). Yet, more than this, as Dickens wrote in a letter to a friend, these events moved him passionately. He defended the Italian revolutionaries:

Like you, I shudder at the distresses that come of these unavailing risings; my blood runs hotter . . . at the thought of the leaders safe and the instruments perishing by hundreds; yet what is to be done? Their wrongs are so great that they *will* rise from time to time somehow. It would be to doubt the eternal providence of God, to doubt that they will rise successfully at last. . . . Think if you and I were Italians . . . could we be better than these men? Should we be so good? I should not, I am afraid, if I know myself.

Thus *A Tale of Two Cities* is about revolution in general, not just the French Revolution; the interplay of his attraction and revulsion from violence is once again part of its whole scheme; and no-one who reads his letter of 3 February 1860 to Henry Fothergill Chorley (1802-72) can doubt it. 'If it were not a living reality to me,' he explained, he could not have expressed himself so forcibly.

The theme is worked out in terms of the two cities, the two heroes (Darnay and Carton), and both through a traditional resolution in the marriage of Citizen Manette's daughter to the heir of oppressive aristocrats and in the Christian self-sacrifice of the apparently 'worthless' Carton to save Darnay.

The novel is made in an intricate pattern of opposites. Some elements in the plot, are too intricate, particularly the spy-story and Jeremy Cruncher's 'body snatching'. Yet they are carried out with spirit; and, beneath the grotesque and even comic action, they join in giving the sense that characters and events are driven by hidden forces. Dickens writes of powerful human impulses released by the long-suppressed revolution, and of 'the wonders' that he writes, 'all of us have . . . hidden in our breasts, only needing circumstances to evoke them'. So certain figures and incidents are multiplied and deepen the effects, one of which is a sense of the mystery of life.

The pattern of the novel is also linked with a faith in social regeneration. Even in the darkest scenes there is the suggestion of a brighter future in which 'the evil of this time' will be 'gradually making expiation for itself and wearing out'. It is not only to be found in Carton's final vision. Each of the three men grouped round Lucie Manette is 'recalled to life'. Her father gains his release from the Bastille; her husband's life is restored by his deliverance from the revolutionary prison; and Carton finds his by death. As he paces the Paris streets before taking Darnay's place at the guillotine, the words of the burial service persistently come to his mind: 'I am the Resurrection and the Life, saith the Lord: he that believeth in me, though he were dead, yet he shall live.' They come back to him; and, as he faces death, recur not just as a pious ending but as a vital expression of the Christian ethic of self-sacrifice which has been steadily contrasted with revolutionary savagery.

In the preface Dickens called attention to his belief that the work somehow expressed his own experience. It is likely that he had his association with Ellen Ternan in mind, through the performance in *The Frozen Deep*; but he possibly meant much more than this. The prefaces have a way of meaning more than they apparently say. We have already seen how strongly Dickens identified with the revolutionary side, and he may have identified himself with Dr Manette and Carton, who suffer imprisonment and rejection. When Manette is in despair he is like Dickens in his compulsive need for action, for it was 'the character of his mind to be always in singular need of occupation'. We know him as someone of 'great firmness of purpose, strength of resolution, and vigour of action' – as a man who is aware of a 'suppression always shut up within him'.

Dickens also divides himself between Carton and Darnay. As Carton gazes into the mirror, he sees in Darnay all that he might have been, and, similarly we are shown Carton as the man who has 'fallen away from' all that Darnay is. So Dickens identifies with all three and perhaps with all the characters in the story; and possibly with none more than the father, for at this time he still meant to keep to the declaration in the 'Violated Letter' in which he said of Ellen that she was as 'innocent and pure, and as good as my own dear daughters'.

The Christian symbols used throughout the novel may be thought partly inappropriate. They are borrowed for a purpose not purely Christian, to express not the resurrection of man or Christ but to communicate the wonder of life. For example, when waiting for their execution, we see Carton and the seamstress standing 'in the fast-thinning throng of victims . . . as if they were alone. Eye to eye, voice to voice, hand to hand, heart to heart, these two children of the Universal Mother, else so wide apart and differing, have come together on the dark highway, to repair home together, and to rest in her bosom'. Then her number is called, and 'the murmuring of many voices, the pressing of so many footsteps on the outskirts of the crowd, so that it swells forward in a mass, like one great heave of water, all flashes away'. She passes to a land where Carton tells her there is 'no Time' and 'no trouble'. The emphasis of the scene is on the mystery of love and sacrifice – of *human* love and sacrifice. Carton prophesies of himself that he will survive in the memory of Lucie and her child. The rest is a mystery.

Once again, what is holy in life is shown in terms of romantic love. Carton lays down his life for Lucie rather than Darnay. As he parts from the seamstress, 'she kisses his lips; he kisses hers; they solemnly bless each other'. When Madame Defarge finally faces Miss Pross, hate confronts love, and 'love, always so much stronger than hate', triumphs. Lucie's love overcomes fear when she first meets her resurrected father; and his restoration begins as they embrace and 'his cool white head' mingles 'with her radiant hair', which warms and lights it 'as though it were the light of Freedom shining on him'. Love, standing for all the forces of life, lasting power and goodness is shown to be as strange and wonderful as the steps which lead Madame Defarge to her fate, as the ways by which the hidden account of the prisoner of the Bastille comes to light, as the first meeting of Carton and Darnay or the reunion of Miss Pross and her brother Solomon, and as the essentially 'profound secret and mystery' of 'every human creature . . . to every other' (Chapter 3).

For all its weaknesses, the story evokes this sense of wonder and is told with tautness and power. Certainly almost everything comes to depend on the narrative and Dickens's way of telling it. It was a bold experiment, some of the interest of which depends on what he reached out for rather than what he achieved.

Chapter 12

Great Expectations

AT GAD'S HILL Dickens played at being a country squire, cutting himself off from London society and making new friends. Then, one day in 1860, after reading the story of some eminent man, he put much of his past on the bonfire, gathering together most of his old papers and letters to burn them in a field at the back of the house. As they went up in flames, he remarked, 'Would to God every letter I have ever written was on that pile.' The great continuing Pilgrim edition of his letters is now gathering together all that remains, and revealing his stature in a way that was previously hard even to imagine. Even outside his fiction his writing is remarkable, and he cannot really be known as an author unless his readers venture beyond the novels.

About the same time, he had begun a new series in *All the Year Round* entitled *The Uncommercial Traveller*, often vivid and powerful essays like those in *Household Words*. Yet, when the first edition appeared in 1861, they appeared extraordinarily sombre. The first was about a terrible shipwreck, while others dealt with workhouses, the police, sick soldiers, tramps, night walks and the Paris morgue. The dark side of Dickens's later work is sometimes exaggerated but here it is almost unrelieved.

It was while writing one of them that he found 'such a fine, new grotesque idea', that he promptly put it aside for a book. 'It so opens out before me,' he wrote to Forster, 'that I can see the whole of a serial revolving upon it, in a most singular and comic manner.'

He began it as a monthly serial, but was soon called to the rescue of *All the Year Round*, and set to work. With the first three weekly numbers he introduced a boy and a convict, Pip and Magwitch, 'the pivot on which the story will turn . . . the grotesque, tragi-comic conception that first encouraged me'. Joe Gargery, the blacksmith, was brought in, with Wopsle and Pumblechook, making the opening 'droll': 'I have put a child and a good-natured foolish man in relations that seem to me very funny.' Altogether, he assured Forster, 'you will not have to complain of the want of humour as in the Tale of Two Cities'.

Dickens's refusal to repeat the early novels had become a common complaint. Miss Coutts even worried that he was beginning to show his unhappiness in his writing, and this *did* disturb him. Anxious to vindicate his work, he hastily replied: 'As to my art, I have as great a delight in it as the most enthusiastic of my readers; and the sense of my responsibility in that wise, is always upon me when I take pen in hand. If *I* were soured, I should still try to sweeten the lives and fancies of others, but I am not – not at all.' It is a disturbing comment.

The more we are told about his 'intentions' the less easy it often seems to understand them. No doubt we have to see Dickens as someone purposefully writing an optimistic story to keep up the sales of his magazine. He may even have felt that his eventual opening was pleasantly humorous as well as 'grotesque'. What is more, he was making use of his old understanding (often imparted to contributors) that humour could 'enhance and intensify' his work. Unquestionably he was a moralist. And we have to grasp all this if we are to sense other forces which are no less surely (if less clearly) moving within the work. But, with *Great Expectations*, there is a challenging variety of ways in which it can be read, some of which are mutually exclusive.

It is the fundamental irony of the work that helps to make this possible: it is a tragi-comedy from the start. The first three numbers are, in fact, good-humoured, but the approach is new. Once more, the story begins on Christmas Eve. Yet there is not a flake of snow in sight, not a robin on the bough nor a turkey on the table: only the cold mist on the marshes, an escaped convict in the churchyard and a gibbet looming over the flats. There are no carols; Pip says he has gone to hear them, but he lies. Stirring the pudding makes his arm ache. There are no bells, no Christmas games. Just a good dinner interrupted by soldiers searching for the convict.

Except in Pip and Joe there is no charity or goodwill, though Pumblechook passes a bottle round with such joviality that he seems to forget that he has just presented it to Mrs Joe: 'As I watched them,' says Pip, 'enjoying themselves so much, I thought what a terrible good sauce for a dinner my fugitive friend on the marshes was. They had not enjoyed themselves a quarter so much, before the entertainment was brightened with the excitement he furnished.' We are warned that as well as having freshness and novelty the work is to show – and ask for – a new insight.

Of course, one man's insight may be another's recognition of the obvious. To G. B. Shaw, for example, 'Pip, like his creator, has no religion. . . . Pip never prays, and church means nothing to him but Mr Wopsle's orotundity'. But this is not true. We are thrice told he prays when Orlick has him trapped in the old sluice-house on the marshes. Christian behaviour and worldly behaviour are constantly contrasted. When Pip and Joe go to church after burning Pip's indentures (Chapter 19) Pip crassly thinks that 'perhaps the clergyman would not have read that about the rich man and the kingdom of Heaven, if he had known all'. At his sister's funeral, he notices that the fatuous Pumblechook coughs 'reservations', when 'those noble passages were read which remind humanity how it brought nothing into the world and can take nothing out, and how it 'fleeth like a shadow'. Joe Gargery is even forced on our attention, as a Christian. When he says good-bye as Pip leaves the forge, 'And so GOD bless you, dear old Pip, old chap, GOD bless you!' – Pip says he thought, 'The fashion of his dress could no more come in its way when he spoke these words, than it would come in its way in Heaven.' And when he finds that Joe has been nursing him in his fever, Pip penitently breaks out, 'O God bless him! O God bless this gentle Christian man!'. In his simplicity and goodness, and in his love for children, Joe is of the Kingdom of Heaven – though, in other ways, we might have some slight reservations about Joe just as Pumblechook has about his Prayer-Book.

We shall have to ask ourselves who is saying this. For it is all certainly present. The self-seeking Pockets are not named by accident, and when they discuss the outspoken Matthew:

> 'Poor dear soul!' said the lady, with an abruptness of manner quite my sister's. 'Nobody's enemy but his own!' . . .
> 'Cousin Raymond,' observed another lady, 'we are to love our neighbour.'
> 'Sarah Pocket,' returned Cousin Raymond, 'if a man is not his own neighbour, who is?'

'Beggar my Neighbour', is the game Pip and Estella play in front of Miss Havisham in the old house, and it all brings us back to Dickens's favourite parable.

There are other 'moralities'. It is also the story of several minds that have shut themselves away from ordinary life only to corrupt. Satis House stands for them all. In his last interview with Miss Havisham, Pip sees that 'in shutting out the light of day, she had shut out infinitely more; that in seclusion, she had secluded herself from a thousand natural and healing influences; that her mind, brooding solitary, had grown diseased, as all minds must and do and will that reverse the appointed order of their Maker'. Therefore, what is natural and good, is right.

Miss Havisham's vengeance on the world brings a desolation on herself; and it is the same with Estella and other characters. Yet, in the end, the emphasis is all on forgiveness. After the scene when Pip tells Estella and Miss Havisham that he has discovered his benefactor at last, Estalla is always to remember that Pip said 'God bless you and God forgive you'. In the interview just before her death Miss Havisham begs Pip's forgiveness, and he answers 'I want forgiveness and direction too much to be bitter with you'. As she lies dying, her last words are, 'Take the pencil and write under my name, "I forgive her".' Throughout his last 'stage' Pip grows to realise how much everyone needs forgiveness, until at the end he begs Joe and Biddy, 'as you have been to church today, and are in charity and love with all mankind', to forget his faults and to forgive him.

The emphasis is all on the Christian virtues of charity and forgiveness. Even Magwitch takes his part, when (right out of character) he rises in court when condemned by the Judge, to say: 'My Lord, I have received my sentence of Death from the Almighty, but I bow to yours.' The sun strikes through the great windows sending 'a broad shaft of light' between those condemned and the Judge, 'linking both together, and perhaps reminding some among the audience, how both were passing on . . . to the greater Judgement that knoweth all things and cannot err'. And, as Magwitch lies dying, Pip tells him of his daughter and how she is now 'a lady and very beautiful'; then, thinking of their reading of the New Testament: 'I thought of the two men who went up into the Temple to pray, and I knew there were no better words that I could say beside his bed, than "O Lord, be merciful to him a sinner!"' It is the same Magwitch who carried about with him a greasy black Testament 'solely to swear people on in cases of emergency'.

The mood is also a searching examination of a society in which, as Karl Marx (1818-83) said, 'the sordid cash nexus is the chief bond between man and man'. As perhaps most readers see, the novel is a study of class and the power of money. Pip thinks that money can do anything, and Magwitch absurdly believes in its power. He throws his greasy bursting wallet on the table:

> 'There's something worth spending in that there book, dear boy. It's yourn. . . . I've come to the old country fur to see my gentleman spend his money *like* a gentleman. That'll be *my* pleasure. . . . And blast you all!' he wound up, looking round the room and snapping his fingers once with a loud snap, 'blast you every one, from the judge in his wig, to the colonist a-stirring up the dust, I'll show you a better gentleman that the whole kit on you put together!'

The work is certainly written for a particular culture, addressed to readers of its own time. The ironies about money in a Christian society were ripe for a world in which an Attorney-General would address a YMCA meeting saying that he was 'perfectly confident that the principle of mutual benevolence, of a universal desire to do good, derived from Christianity . . . is one of the best and most sure modes of securing even temporary success in life (Cheers)'.

We have probably learned to be puzzled by *Great Expectations*. Should we agree with those who think that the novel is almost revolutionary (unlikely): can we regard Pip as totally redeemed by his generosity to Herbert by secretly buying him a partnership? The firm prospers, 'we had a good name, and worked for our profits, and did very well'. If anything in society is seen as diseased it is the criminal class, encouraged by the Law to flourish like a well-tended garden. (Not that Dickens, even then, wanted lenience. 'Dickens and Crime' raises fascinating questions, to which there are many simple answers – usually wrong.) All these questions must, for the moment, be left for self-questioning and answering, as if the reader were not just putting himself in Pip's place but actually able to *be* him and observe him at every age.

The apparent meaning and the inner meanings cannot be disjoined. Yet what has happened with *Great Expectations* is that Dickens has fully devised a fictional world on its own. It is misguided to insist how it 'must' be 'read'. He has reached a stage when he might claim with the French novelist Gustave Flaubert (1821-80) that he has 'cut the umbilical cord'; for, far from identifying with Pip as he narrates his story, he does what Flaubert advised his fellow novelist George Sand (1804-76) to do: 'By an effort of mind, go over to the characters, as it were, not make them come over to us'. In his conception of Pip's telling of his own story, Dickens found a technique of especial subtlety.

It is simple enough in one sense: we can never know quite how far to accept Pip as a reliable narrator. For example, did Dickens know that when Pip quotes St Luke to himself as Magwitch is dying, he is really misquoting in a most revealing way? But then (temporarily cutting our own 'cord' with the author) how far may we read Philip Pirrip, our narrator, as engaged in purposeful self-exposure in his intended penitence, as he clearly is to some degree?

It is, perhaps, usually more rewarding for readers to accept the conventions of the form of the mid-Victorian novel as if they were Victorians themselves. We know, for example, that no autobiographer of this time (or of any time, perhaps?) could have written his work in a shape and form so much like a novel, as that in which David and Pip are supposed to have written theirs. This is itself a fiction that we accept for the sake of certain pleasures and rewards. It is often a dubious exercise to deconstruct or analyse novels of the period. Yet *Great Expectations* stands up to any amount of probing. It is a curious work, being not just Pirrip's story told by himself, but the story of a man accounting for himself in a way which includes self-told accounts of others like himself. In fact, if we re-establish the connection with Dickens, we cannot help thinking that the author of this work is someone who not only started to tell his own autobiography, but who had already recomposed it as fiction not once (in *David Copperfield*), but twice (in *The Haunted Man* as well). But, at last, he has found a form which keeps him close to the reader yet apart, a style of self-reflexive irony, and a way of remembering which keeps us balanced between past, present and future. To call it a 'modern' work would be to under-rate the mid-Victorians.

The division between what Dickens actually said about his own novel and what it implies is unbridgeable: his comments to Lytton about the altered ending are almost fatuous. And though much discussion has centred on such questions as whether we are to think Pip a snob, little attention has been given to what Pip thinks of himself or how this can ever be known. We have heard much about Pip's sense of guilt, sometimes without allowance for the way in which it derives from his own sensitivity. The question is not only whether we should accept the self-contempt in his confession, or perhaps admire his astonishing transformation and willingness to help Magwitch after his first sense of revulsion. It is also how we are to read him (and, of course, how we should read the novel), and whether we do not soon begin to question nearly everything he says once he has been removed from the elementary decencies of Joe.

Even the most acceptable of our interpretations makes less of the novel than it can claim for itself. In advice to a contributor to *All the Year Round* Dickens explained, 'My notion always is, that when I have made the people to play out the play, it is, as it were, their own business to do it, and not mine.' It is much as he said in a speech in praise of Thackeray, that 'every writer of fiction . . . writes in effect for the stage. . . . The truth and wisdom that are in him must permeate the art of which truth and passion are the life'. *Great Expectations* is perhaps the only novel which completely realises this aim.

It is difficult to relinquish discussion of various aspects of the novel, such as Dickens's justified delight in its ingenious construction, his changing attitude to women characters, further ways in which the tale is autobiographical, what the English novelist Graham Greene has called its 'secret prose' written in 'delicate and exact poetic cadences', and Pip's self-consciousness and uncertainty. There can be no doubt of the advances that Dickens had made. Without demanding attention for what was new in the novel, Dickens produced his greatest work only to have it greeted by many critics as a welcome return to his old manner.

He began a new series of public readings outside London in October 1861, delayed until the novel was finished, and these went on at intervals into 1863. Appearance in his own character and reading his own stories, had come to mean far more to him than mere acting; with many to depend on him the money meant much; and, no longer compelled to write, he was making the most of his freedom.

Chapter 13

Our Mutual Friend

THE READINGS WENT ON in the spring of 1863, and at Christmas Dickens wrote *Mrs Lirriper's Lodgings* for *All the Year Round*. Mrs Lirriper is one of the few characters from the later Christmas numbers, who are still remembered. The rest sold well, but she alone says Forster, 'took her place . . . among people known to everybody'. Dickens declared that she was a 'brilliant lady. God bless her!' She reappeared in *Mrs Lirriper's Legacy* (1864), but many readers will prefer *Dr Marigold's Prescriptions* (1866).

Early in 1864 Dickens tried to settle to a new work in monthly numbers, his last complete novel. He had fixed on the title of *Our Mutual Friend* as early as 1861 but, for a while, found nothing new to say. 'Alas!' he wrote a year later, 'I have hit upon nothing for a story. Again and again I have tried.' Seeing that his old inspiration had gone, he decided to keep back the serial until he had five numbers in hand. 'I have grown hard to satisfy,' he said, 'and write very slowly. And I have so much – not fiction – that will be thought of . . . that I am forced to take more care than I once took.'

At first the story was not popular and after only three months he began to fall behind: 'Although I have not been wanting in industry, I have been wanting in invention. This week I have been very unwell . . . and, as I know from two days' slow experience, have a very mountain to climb before I see the open country of my work.' Yet he wrote to his publisher, 'I regard No. 4 as certain to pick up, and I have the strongest faith in the book's doing thoroughly well. I believe it to be GOOD, full of variety and always rising in its working out of the people and the story. (I know I put into it the making of a dozen books.)' But he was depressed and ill.

That spring and summer he felt he would break down if he did not get away, saying as he left for France 'no one knows . . . how near to it I have been'. His crowning misfortune was to be involved in a terrible railway accident on returning in June. He worked for hours among the dead and dying. What made it worse was that he had to look after Ellen Ternan, who had been in the same compartment. When he sat down again at his desk he was sick and faint after writing only a few notes and, for the first time for years, misjudged the length of one of the numbers. He thrust aside his other worries and worked extremely hard; but once the end was in sight told an American publisher that it was

unlikely that he would 'fall to work upon another novel yet awhile'.
Written under such conditions, *Our Mutual Friend* may seem
problematical, showing a sense of strain and lack of coherence in
development. The wheels of the story spin without engaging; the
heavy folds of the nineteen-number novel hang loosely about the
characters and plot which are not expansive enough to fill them out.
Dickens had complained bitterly about weekly serialisation, but under
its discipline had done some of his best work. Now he wrote to Wilkie
Collins that he felt like an amateur actor thrust on the stage of the giant
San Carlo opera house at Naples: 'Strange to say, I felt at first quite lost
at getting back to the large canvas and big brushes.'
Nor is it surprising that sales fell off. The opening would be
extraordinary if we were still to regard him as a family novelist to be
read aloud round the fireside. Gaffer Hexam's work of scavenging
corpses from the Thames is depressing, and Dickens showed little of
his old zest in describing it. Hexam himself is half dead. The
Veneerings are introduced as if they were going to play an important
part, but even this is a deception. We remember Podsnap, because he
is the only one in the Social Chorus who has anything memorable to
say; but Dickens's imagery has often become grotesque rather than
fanciful. There is an uneasy balance between wishing 'to sweeten . . .
the lives of others' (as he told Miss Coutts) and showing a darker side
of life. Yet, even well after he had started, Dickens told Collins that he
meant it to be 'a combination of drollery and romance' – even though
the humour is sometimes forced and the romance kept in check.
There are sharp differences of opinion about the novel which
depend on how it is read, and if we keep that question in mind it is
interesting to compare different readings: not because any one is right
or wrong, but because it changes kinds from novel to romance, satire
or fantasy, or almost in the oral tradition or as a self-questioning quest.
The young Henry James (1843-1916), the future novelist and critic,
reviewed it for *The Nation*, appalled at its being anything other than a
novel. He saw it as wanting in inspiration: '*Bleak House* was forced;
Little Dorrit was laboured; the present work was dug out as with spade
and pickaxe', and congratulated Dickens on 'his success in what we
should call the manufacture of fiction. . . . Seldom, we reflected; had
we read a book so intensely *written*, so little seen, known or felt'. The
characters were superficial and 'essentially small', it recklessly used up
situations that would satisfy a more right-minded novelist for a whole
range of novels and James was outraged at the element of fantasy in
such characters as the dolls' dressmaker Jenny Wren. If *Our Mutual
Friend* were to be read as just a conventional novel the young James
would be right. But then it is quite clear that this cannot be the sole way
to read it.

A wiser review is one that Dickens himself admired, and, though he rarely discussed his books once they were finished, we may get some idea of what he thought of it from what Eneas Sweetland Dallas (1828-79) wrote for *The Times*. Dallas was a journalist and intelligent critic whom Dickens had tried to help in 1865 by recommending him to Lord John Russell (1792-1872) the prime minister, who was responsible for the appointment to the Regius Chair in English Literature at Edinburgh. Soon after, Dallas wrote his review, and it seems that Dickens was so pleased with it and grateful for some other service that he gave Dallas the valuable present of the original manuscript. Anthony Trollope (1815-82), the novelist, expressed disapproval of such transactions; but, as it was the only time Dickens did anything of the kind, we may assume that he was disinterested. The remarkable thing about it is that the review is not entirely favourable. Dallas had some fairly hard things to say about the way in which there was, at first, 'an appearance of great effort without corresponding result'. He thought that:

> The first few chapters . . . are very heavy, and . . . that *Our Mutual Friend* has defects we . . . shall ruthlessly point out. The weak part . . . is to be found in . . . 'The Social Chorus'. This is the title which Mr Dickens gives one of his chapters. . . . We can divide the tale distinctly into two parts, like a Greek drama – one part truly dramatic and given to the evolution of the story . . . the other a sort of social chorus having no real connexion with the tale in which we are interested. Now the idea here is a great one, but it has not been worked out with details of sufficient interest. Of Mr Dickens's main story . . . we cannot speak too highly; it is a masterpiece, but . . . [in writing about the chorus] the novelist has this further difficulty that he has to make us care about people who are remarkable for their nothingness . . . who, by the hypothesis are uninteresting. Now, it is in dealing with this cruel problem that Mr Dickens falls short.

Dallas has much to say in praise of the naturalness of the main story's characters, and he especially extols the novel for its 'immense amount of thought': in the whole work 'there is not a careless line'. Dickens was apparently happy to accept blame as well as praise.

Assessments differ because few readers or critics take the whole novel into account; and it reminds us that the long mid-Victorian novel presents peculiar problems. It is often multi-plotted and multi-styled; different forms are used for different aspects, social satire, simple fable, comic exuberance, oblique insight, descriptions of thoughts and feelings, or passionate and anguished drama such as Headstone's, and so on. Readers admit to bewilderment; critics tend to preserve their confidence by re-creating works according to preference. In re-reading we may all do this; and, if Dickens had made use of this inclination to create a special form, as in the shorter *Great Expectations*, it might have been completely successful. But in certain ways it is overambitious. This is partly why our moral or allegorical interpretations affect our readings: they encourage selectivity and emphasis, helping us to grasp some implications at the cost of missing others.

It may well be read as a study of selfhood expressing a sense of man's precarious place in life, and the nature of his being, in which our attention focuses on the river as a dark centre to life. Gaffer's occupation, Rokesmith's resurrection from the river, Wrayburn's escape from drowning, Headstone's death, Riderhood's and Gaffer's are often less remarkable for mythic potency than because Dickens uses them to say something directly. He does not always say it as well as he does through Jenny Wren (Book 2, Chapter 2; Book 2, Chapter 5). But he certainly sees Rokesmith's strange situation as representative, showing a real side to life and a fanciful one: 'A real side, so difficult that, though I think of it every day, I never thoroughly think it out. . . . I know I evade it, as many men – perhaps most men do evade thinking their way through their greatest perplexity.' In assuming a second identity Rokesmith is compelled to think what his own personality is; and he finds himself at last, as we are told Eugene Wrayburn does. Their self-examinations are matched by others, through their pretences (e.g. Boffin's), conversions (Bella's), a variety of names (Jenny Wren, or the renamed Johnny), acts of deception (Fledgeby or the Lammleses), deceptive outward appearances (the Veneerings or the respectable Headstone), or the curious domestic division of the Boffins (Book 1, Chapter 5), in endless variation. It is all usually worked out better through such a complexity of patterns, than in single instances such as Boffin's miserliness, or the curious 'A Solo and a Duett' (Book 2), with its gauche self-analysis.

The novel is so rich as to need lengthy consideration. We cannot pass by, because it has been noticed before, the magnificent display of not only a Social Chorus singing the praises of money but a society dominated by 'Shares. O mighty Shares!' It is so simple in outline, so sharp in perception and illustration. Some of it might seem to come from Dickens's old stock, but with a new turn and biting emphasis. In hearing about education, we have not previously met the mean ambition to be 'respectable' as displayed by Headstone and Charley Hexam. We see not just the contrast between heart and head but the dramatic confrontation between the schoolmaster and the generous would-be seducer, Eugene. There are clear echoes of the folk- and fairy-tale which, there is reason to think, had been given deeper consideration. The extension of the boundaries of a vividly realised

London to riverside East End, is also something new. The strength of the novel is not in the woven pattern on which Dickens prided himself in the 'Postscript', but in the variety and intensity of its scenes, images and insights: easily said, but it would mean going back to the novel for full illustration.

Without its various obvious designs we would be bewildered; even with them we must wonder. Of course we are right to see it as a study of an acquisitive and possessive society. 'A man may do anything lawful for money,' says the Genius of the Social Chorus. He can buy his way into Parliament, buy a wife, friends and flattery. The Veneerings' gold camels, Podsnap's massive plate, and shares all show society's blatant worship of property and wealth.

As well as these symbols there is another dominating the whole book: the great dust-heaps. They have their place on the monthly cover and in the frontispiece to the second volume; and apart from the age-old significance of muck as wealth, there are many references to Dust which show a special meaning. It is argued by those who believe in the book's consistency that it stands for wealth, 'the supreme goal of nineteenth-century society', and ultimately the dust and ashes of all misdirected effort in a world in which true values have been distorted by an all-pervading greed for money.

All true. The only objection is that this chief symbol is used ambiguously. The foul dust-heap represents riches; but its more unsavoury aspects are glossed over whatever may have been said about them later. Second, we are not allowed to forget that the golden-hearted Boffin helped to built them up, he then inherits them, and they are passed on to Bella and John. If any deduction is to be drawn from this ending it is that there is no objection to inheriting wealth without working for it, and it is wrong for a man like old Harmon to build it up by providing a service for the community. This is obviously absurd. The image is misapplied. Yet it is made perfectly clear that when the happy pair come into their inheritance and drive up to their new home, we are meant to be as delighted as the Boffins.

On this interpretation the book is flawed and the ending slightly ridiculous. As John and Bella enter the new house and ascend the stairs, they find them 'tastefully ornamented with the most beautiful flowers. . . . Going on a little higher, they came to a charming aviary, in which a number of tropical birds were flying about; and among those birds were gold and silver fish . . . and a fountain, and all manner of wonders'. They look all over it: 'And a dainty house it was, and a tastefully beautiful. . . . And on Bella's exquisite toilette-table was an ivory casket, and in the casket were jewels the like of which she had never dreamed of.' *Tastefully* is overworked throughout.

Clearly this is not how it should be read, but we are drawn to this interpretation. The story is really another 'morality', to which we are meant to apply the Ruskinian teaching of *Unto This Last*: that is, of the New Testament parable of the workers in the vineyard. The unearned wealth of 'great expectations' is now shown to be as good as, or better than, Pip's working 'for our profits'. The angle is new, yet the view is the same: that someone's worth is what matters, not class or money or other criteria.

We might also criticise the relation of John and Bella and even Eugene and Lizzie. The latter has an obvious special meaning; in fact it is nearly all meaning. It shows again that money does not matter and that love does; and even that someone who feels purposeless may find a new determination through a girl of the people. It balances uneasily between 'fancy' and reality. Had this been thoroughly worked out as a criticism of society, through the characters, the novel might have had the explosive force that some wish to find in it. But it is true in more ways than one that (as Forster says of Betty Higden and the Poor Law) *Our Mutual Friend* finishes what *Oliver Twist* began. Headstone takes the place of Sikes; the Jew, Riah, is an apology for Fagin; and Oliver's function as 'the principle of Good' is taken over by Lizzie. Yet in too many ways the later novel is also much more insistently realistic, self-conscious and profound; it feels contemporary, its characters speak more naturally, its scenes are familiar, and so the allegory and fantasy are harder to accept. Apart from this, the function that had been fitting for a child-figure is false for the woman to whom Headstone says, 'You draw me to you. If I were shut up in a strong prison, you would draw me out. I should break through the wall to come to you. If I were lying on a sick bed, you would draw me up – to stagger to your feet and fall there.' For, forcibly projected as Headstone is, and intriguing as Wrayburn may be, Lizzie is weak as a representation of her sex and class. The attempted organisation and sophistication of the novel no longer quite match Dickens's emphatic style, his intensely vital scenes and characters, or its appeal to 'fancy' in such figures as the Dolls' Dressmaker and the Golden Dustman. After a quarter of a century of development, Dickens was now pushing his aims beyond his means.

But the achievement is remarkable. No single statement sums up the novel; it is varied and complex enough to invite enthusiasm. Its detail is finer than ever, if not so unforced. It is an analysis of society, a romantic justification of humanity, a fierce comment on contemporary life, and an attempt to express Dickens's self-understanding. The emphasis of any one of these to the exclusion of the others is a distortion. As a study of the times it is doubtful whether it should be read just as an indictment of contemporary society, though the anxiety about such people as the Veneerings and the world of Shares was a topical issue, as we can see from specific articles in *All the Year Round*. Dickens, however, did not object so much to wealth as to dishonesty, and he wanted to show that a love of money could corrupt a whole society. It is partly brought out at the end of the chapter when John and Bella arrive at their new house. The Boffins gaze at Bella and her baby:

'It looks as if the old man's spirit had found rest at last; don't it?' said Mrs Boffin. . . . 'And as if his money had turned bright again, after a long, long rust in the dark, and was at last a-beginning to sparkle in the sunlight.'

All is well now. The money can be put to good use, because it is in good hands. A simple theme in a complex novel, which is not least intriguing if we begin to try to relate the way its author looks at life, to the life he was then leading.

Chapter 14

Last years and
Edwin Drood

YET MORE PUBLIC READINGS followed, but Dickens was beginning to suffer bouts of ill-health, though so far nothing serious had been diagnosed. One reading series led on to another, and at sixty pounds a night for forty-two nights, he was almost reaching the magnificent sum Thackeray had forecast of £20,000 a year.

This is a period of his life of which relatively little is known. When not appearing in public, Dickens possibly spent much of his time with Ellen; and they may have shared an interest in perfecting the readings. We cannot be sure exactly what their relations were. Years later, after she had married, she is alleged to have said that she loathed the thought of their intimacy, but whether this was just in retrospect or even faithfully reported is unknown.

Like all these biographical 'details', it is not unimportant. We are all aware of the relations between the author and his work, and none more so than Dickens himself. It genuinely looks as if the greatest public figure of the age often delighted to escape to the domestic privacy of Peckham or Slough. The sentimentalist about money rejoiced in earning it. We are compelled to see Dickens as constantly seeking to escape from a life in which he must have felt he was playing a part, and yet showing amazing self-command so as to avoid having to go the way the world wanted. It may have been as demanding as his public performances and as skilful.

Yet in spite of the darker nature of his writings, such friends as George Dolby (his new reading-manager) report him 'always cheerful and good-humoured' when on tour, even 'in the most trying situations', and a delightful host with a never-failing radiance that made 'the most ordinary things in life' seem 'special in his presence'. The Duke of Devonshire wrote in his diary, in 1851, after seeing Dickens about a charity performance, 'I am bewitched by him'. Richard Watson, his neighbour for five months in 1846, remarked that: 'It is impossible to describe the feelings of regard and friendship with which he has inspired us. He is certainly the most natural, unaffected, distinguished man I have ever met.' Sir George Russell wrote, 'As a charming companion, I never knew his equal,' and the American critic Charles Eliot Norton (1827-1908), 'I never knew a famous and flattered man so utterly unhurt by it all. . . . The better one knew him, the more one loved him.'

Such unfailing praise may sometimes have annoyed those who never knew him, but others who thought they disliked him found him irresistible. Trollope, no admirer, wrote, 'Of the general charm of his manner I despair of giving any idea . . . he warmed the social atmosphere with that summer glow which seemed to attend him'.

A great tribute was paid to him in 1867 when he was given a farewell dinner before his second visit to the United States for further readings. Nearly four hundred and fifty guests attended, Lytton took the chair, and, for once, Dickens was almost overcome when he rose to reply. At the end of his speech he explained that as well as fulfilling a professional engagement he went to America to renew acquaintance with 'a kind, large-hearted, generous and great people'. He sailed a week later.

Before leaving he arranged that Ellen should follow him there if practicable. It soon become clear that this was impossible. Yet the readings themselves were all that he had hoped for, except that as he went on they took a toll of his health. Towards the end, he wrote, 'I am nearly used up. Climate, distance, catarrh, travelling, and hard work, have begun . . . to tell heavily on me', and his old lameness came back. Yet Dolby says that he never once complained. Before leaving, he was given a banquet by the New York Press in which he expressed his thanks for a reception of 'unsurpassable politeness, delicacy, sweet temper, hospitality' and consideration.

After his return, friends noticed a 'manifest abatement of his natural force', as Forster wrote, 'the elasticity of his bearing was impaired, and the wonderful brightness of his eye was dimmed'. The photographic record of his last years (almost never reproduced by biographers) shows how greatly he had aged. Though Dickens lived longer than some of his sons and brothers, almost everyone connected with the readings (including doctors) thought that they shortened his life. Yet he still refused advice. He again assumed control of *All the Year Round* while Wills was ill, and agreed to give a series of a hundred readings for £8,000. He meant it to be the last, and it was.

It would be wrong to suppose that he acted in this way just because of a desire for money, security or applause. They played their part: he enjoyed performing, and some of his anxiety for the future was justified. He was afraid that even before his death some of his family might go back to the shiftless ways of their grandfather. Charley had already been bankrupt, and other sons were showing signs of the family failing in ways not published even now. Thackeray had had the same wish to provide for his family by giving readings. It was a brute fact that many of Dickens's friends (including Mark Lemon, Douglas

Jerrold, Leigh Hunt, James Sheridan Knowles) accepted charity or left their families unprovided for. George Dolby died in a workhouse. In order to make a special impact on his last appearance he now prepared the reading 'Sikes and Nancy', leading up to the murder-scene. It was tremendous: fainting women were carried out by the dozen, and Macready called it 'two Macbeths'. But it was fatal to his health. The crisis came at the end of April 1869, when the tour was suspended. Even so, by August, he was chairman at a dinner to a visiting Harvard rowing crew; and Robert Lytton, the novelist's son, wrote to him that he had 'rarely felt more genuine pleasure' than in reading his speech, 'the only utterance I have heard addressed in England to listeners in America . . . which has surpassed my ideal', when the general tone about America was usually so mischievous. In September Dickens addressed a great audience in Birmingham on education, winding up with the Delphic remark about his 'faith in the people governing being on the whole, infinitesimal'; his faith in 'the People governed . . . on the whole illimitable'. A 'touch of Radicalism', he said, which he saw 'with pride' made 'the regular political traders of all sorts perfectly mad'.

The final series of readings was in London, and at the last one in March 1870, he announced that he would henceforth devote himself exclusively to writing. He hoped that in two weeks' time his hearers would join in new readings at home of his next novel *Edwin Drood*. 'But from these garish lights I vanish now for evermore, with a heartfelt, grateful, respectful and affectionate farewell.'

The story was to be a *Mystery*, and few of the hints he is said to have dropped about it are to be trusted. It was to be in twelve monthly parts of the usual length; and the first number appeared in April when Dickens told an American friend, with enthusiastic inaccuracy, that the sale had '*very, very far outstripped every one of its predecessors*'.

Though it is hard, in thinking of his last years, not to be influenced by foreknowledge of his death, Dickens himself seems to have had no foreboding until almost the end. If ill, he was still full of life. But the fact that he died when the book was less than half finished (on publication it was *stretched* to fill six numbers) means that critical attention has been concentrated on how the story would have ended.

We can ignore the complexities of plot. The writing itself does not show Dickens at his best; and if the novel could have made its full effect it would have been through novelty of plot and ideas. In John Jasper, Dickens showed an opium-eating, mesmeric murderer with a double consciousness, which allowed him to be among those who hunted himself down. He was certainly connected with the East where he may have learned the art of murder from the Thugs. Edwin Drood is his nephew, and it is possible that the twins, Neville and Helena Landless (from Ceylon), would have been revealed as close relatives. He has a much closer connection with the opium-woman than that of a client. None of this can now be fully worked out.

Dickens's part-plans tell us that the 'key note' was connected with the biblical text (Ezekiel 18:27), 'When the wicked man turneth away from his wickedness . . . he shall save his soul alive', and, in context, Ezekiel teaches that what a man does is his own responsibility, and that he cannot lay the blame on his fathers. A murderer shall 'surely die', but if his son is honest 'he shall not die for the iniquity of his father', but 'shall surely live'. Ezekiel's teaching is that God is just as well as forgiving, and this is Dickens's teaching in several of the novels, for example in the relation between Magwitch and Estella or the Harmons, father and son, in *Our Mutual Friend*. Some such development in the evolution of the plot is likely; and no-one can reasonably believe that, at this stage, Dickens would have relied mainly on mere incident.

Similarly it must also have been meant as a study of goodness and evil; for, as Dickens explained in Chapter 20, Jasper was to be a realistic study of an abnormal criminal, a class that always fascinated him, especially in the way that such men often have a strange power over women; this was something he had returned to not long before in Julius Slinkton, of the short story 'Hunted Down'. Undoubtedly these aspects would have been powerfully developed in the second half of the tale if the exigencies of the plot permitted it.

For Dickens himself the end came suddenly. All day on 8 June he worked on the novel. At dinner he felt ill and fell to the floor. Georgina Hogarth (his sister-in-law) sent for Ellen Ternan and for the children; he lived through the night, and died on 9 June 1870.

Those closest to him were deeply shocked. His elder daughter, Mamie, wrote to her Bostonian friend, Susan Norton: 'You know how beautiful he was in life, & he was most grand and splendid in death. But he is never dead to us. . . . Life can never be the same to us as it has been, and our hearts are very sad and desolate. Every body loved him, but nobody knows what he was to us.' Forster wrote to Susan's father, Charles Eliot Norton: 'To you only I say this, my dear Norton. I have not been able, nor shall be, to have speech on these matters with any one. And to you for the present I will only further say that nothing in the future can, to me, ever again be as it was. The duties of life remain while life remains, but for me the joy is gone for ever more.'

His death was felt as a national calamity. One of the less reverent members of his editorial staff later said, 'He had Westminster Abbey always before him.' He was buried there on 14 June. Benjamin Jowett (1817-93), the liberal-minded Master of Balliol, paid tribute to him at a special service:

Men of genius are different from what we suppose them to be; they have greater pleasure and greater pains, greater affections and greater temptations . . . and . . . can never be altogether understood by their fellow-men. . . . We can hardly calculate the debt of gratitude which is due to a writer who has led us to sympathize with the good, true, sincere, honest English characters of ordinary life, and to laugh at the egotism, the hypocrisy, the false respectability of religious professors and others. . . . He whose loss we now mourn occupied a greater space than any other writer in the minds of Englishmen during the last thirty-five years.

Select bibliography

WORKS BY DICKENS:

Novels

Date of publication in volume form: *Pickwick Papers* (1837); *Oliver Twist* (1838); *Nicholas Nickleby* (1839); *Master Humphrey's Clock*, including *The Old Curiosity Shop* (1841) and *Barnaby Rudge* (1841); *Martin Chuzzlewit* (1844); *Dombey and Son* (1848); *David Copperfield* (1850); *Bleak House* (1853); *Hard Times* (1854); *Little Dorrit* (1857); *A Tale of Two Cities* (1859); *Great Expectations* (1861); *Our Mutual Friend* (1865); *The Mystery of Edwin Drood* (1870). Editions hardly matter except for advanced students, but the definitive Clarendon editions, Oxford, should be consulted, 6 vols (1966 – in progress), general eds. Kathleen Tillotson and James Kinsley. Those published so far are *Oliver Twist* (ed. Tillotson, 1966), *Martin Chuzzlewit* (ed. M. Cardwell, 1982), *Dombey and Son* (ed. A. Horsman, 1974), *David Copperfield* (ed. N. Burgis, 1981), *Little Dorrit* (ed. H. P. Sucksmith, 1979), *Edwin Drood* (ed. M. Cardwell, 1972).

Short stories, essays and sketches

Sunday Under Three Heads, by 'Timothy Sparks', pseud. (1836); *Sketches by Boz*, 1st and 2nd series (1836); *Reprinted Pieces*, articles from *Household Words* (1858); *Christmas Stories* from Christmas numbers of *Household Words* and *All the Year Round* (1850-67); 'Hunted Down', short story (1859); *The Uncommercial Traveller*, essays from *All the Year Round* (1861), added to in later editions; 'George Silverman's Explanation', short story (1868); *Miscellaneous Papers*, collected journalism, ed. B.W. Matz, vols 35, 36 of the Gadshill edition of the *Works*, Chapman & Hall, London; Charles Scribner's Sons, New York, 1906, also published separately and in certain editions of the works; *The Uncollected Writings of Charles Dickens in Household Words*, ed. Harry Stone, 2 vols, Indiana University Press, Bloomington, Indiana, 1969; Allen Lane, London, 1968. See also the *Contributor's Book* for *Household Words*, ed. Anne Lohrli, University of Toronto Press, Toronto, 1973 and a selection, ed. Deborah A. Thomas, *Charles Dickens, Selected Short Fiction*, Penguin Books, Harmondsworth, 1976.

Christmas Books

A Christmas Carol (1843); *The Chimes* (1844); *The Cricket on the Hearth* (1845); *The Battle of Life* (1846); *The Haunted Man* (1848).

Travel

American Notes (1842); *Pictures from Italy* (1846); *The Lazy Tour of Two Idle Apprentices*, with Wilkie Collins (1857).

Miscellaneous

A Child's History of England (1852-4); *The Life of Our Lord*, Associated Newspaper Press, London, 1934, written for Dickens's children and not meant for publication; *The Speeches of Charles Dickens*, ed. K.J. Fielding, Clarendon Press, Oxford, 1960; *Charles Dickens, The Public Readings*, ed. Philip Collins, Clarendon Press, Oxford, 1975; *Charles Dickens' Book of Memoranda*, ed. Fred Kaplan, New York Public Library, New York, 1981.

Dickens as editor

Dickens edited *Bentley's Miscellany* (January, 1837–February 1839); the *Daily News* (21 January–9 February 1846); *Household Words* (1850-9); *All the Year Round* (1859-1870); and separate works including *The Memoirs of Grimaldi* (1837).

Letters

The Letters of Charles Dickens, Pilgrim edn, Clarendon Press, Oxford, 1965– in progress, ed. by Madeline House, Graham Storey, Kathleen Tillotson and others: 5 vols, up to 1849, have appeared (1985). The *Letters*, vols. 10, 11, 12, in The Nonesuch Dickens, Nonesuch Press, London, 1938, span the life but are incomplete and not easily available.

WORKS ABOUT DICKENS

Biography

The best biographies are John Forster, *The Life of Charles Dickens*, 3 vols, Chapman & Hall, London, 1872-4, often reprinted, and ed. by J.W.T. Ley, Cecil Palmer, London, Doubleday, Doran, New York, 1928, and by A.J. Hoppé, J.M. Dent (Everyman), London, 1966; and

Edgar Johnson, *Charles Dickens, His Tragedy and Triumph*, 2 vols, Simon & Schuster, New York, 1952; Gollancz, London, 1953; revised edn, Penguin Books, Harmondsworth, 1977, and Viking Press, New York, 1977. Other useful biographies are Christopher Hibbert, *The Making of Charles Dickens*, Longman, London, 1967, and Norman and Jeanne MacKenzie, *Dickens, A Life*, Oxford University Press, Oxford, 1979.

Biography and criticism have often been combined as in George Gissing, *Charles Dickens, A Critical Study*, Blackie, London, 1898; G.K. Chesterton, *Charles Dickens*, Methuen, London, 1906; Steven Marcus, *Dickens from Pickwick to Dombey*, Chatto & Windus, London, 1964; Basic Books, New York, 1965; K.J. Fielding, *Charles Dickens, A Critical Introduction*, Longman, London, 1965; Sylvère Monod, *Dickens the Novelist*, University of Oklahoma Press, Norman, Oklahoma, 1968; Angus Wilson, *The World of Charles Dickens*, Secker & Warburg, London, 1970; and Harland S. Nelson, *Charles Dickens*, Twayne Publishers, Boston, 1981.

Collected critical essays

Students at all levels will find selective reading in various collections of essays particularly valuable. Such collections include: *Dickens and the Twentieth Century*, ed. J. Gross and G. Pearson, Routledge & Kegan Paul, London, 1962; *The Dickens Critics*, ed. G.H. Ford and Lauriat Lane Jr., Cornell University Press, Ithaca, New York, 1961; *Dickens*, ed. Martin Price, Twentieth Century Views series, Prentice-Hall, Englewood Cliffs, New Jersey, 1967, and a further volume in the same series, *Charles Dickens, New Perspectives*, ed. Wendell Stacy Johnson, 1982; *Charles Dickens; a Penguin Critical Anthology*, ed. Stephen Wall, Penguin Books, Harmondsworth, 1970. See also G.H. Ford, *Dickens and His Readers, Aspects of Novel-Criticism since 1836*, Princeton University Press, Princeton, 1955, and the *Dickens* volume ed. by Philip Collins, in the Critical Heritage series, Routledge & Kegan Paul, London, 1970.

Critical works and special studies

ADRIAN, ARTHUR A.: *Georgina Hogarth and the Dickens Circle*, Oxford University Press, London 1957.

AXTON, WILLIAM F.: *Circle of Fire: Dickens' Vision and Style and the Popular Victorian Theatre*, University of Kentucky Press, Lexington, 1966.

BAGEHOT, WALTER: 'Charles Dickens', *Literary Studies*, 2 vols, Longman, London, 1879

BARNARD, ROBERT: *Imagery and Theme in the Novels of Charles Dickens*, Universitetsforlaget, Bergen, Oslo and Tromsö, 1974.

BROWNE, EDGAR: *Dickens and Phiz*, James Nisbet, London, 1913.

BUTT, JOHN and TILLOTSON, KATHLEEN: *Dickens at Work*, Methuen, London, 1957.

CAREY, JOHN: *The Violent Effigy: A Study of Dickens's Imagination*, Faber & Faber, London, 1973; also published as *Here Comes Dickens: The Imagination of a Novelist*, Schoken, New York, 1974.

CHESTERTON, G.K.: *Charles Dickens*, Methuen, London, 1906.

COCKSHUT, A.O.J.: *The Imagination of Charles Dickens*, Collins, London, 1961.

COHEN, JANE R.: *Dickens and His Original Illustrators*, Ohio State University Press, Columbus, 1980.

COLLINS, PHILIP: *Dickens and Crime*, Macmillan, London, 1962.

—— : *Dickens and Education*, Macmillan, London, 1963.

—— : *Dickens, Interviews and Recollections*, 2 vols, Macmillan, London, 1981.

COOLIDGE JR, ARCHIBALD C.: *Charles Dickens as Serial Novelist*, Iowa State University Press, Ames, 1967.

DALESKI, H.M.: *Dickens and the Art of Analogy*, Faber & Faber, London, 1970.

DAVIS, EARLE R.: *The Flint and the Flame: The Artistry of Charles Dickens*, University of Missouri Press, Columbia, 1963.

DEVRIES, DUANE: *Dickens's Apprentice Years: The Making of a Novelist*, Barnes & Noble, New York, 1976.

DICKENS, MARY: *Charles Dickens by His Eldest Daughter*, Cassell, London, 1885, publ. again as *My Father as I Recall Him*, Roxburghe Press, London, 1897.

DOLBY, GEORGE: *Charles Dickens as I Knew Him*, Fisher Unwin, London, 1885.

DYSON, A.E.: *The Inimitable Dickens: A Reading of the Novels*, Macmillan, London, 1970.

ENGEL, MONROE: *The Maturity of Dickens*, Oxford University Press, London; Harvard University Press, Cambridge, Mass., 1959.

GARIS, ROBERT: *The Dickens Theatre: A Reassessment of the Novels*, Clarendon Press, Oxford, 1965.

GOLDBERG, MICHAEL: *Dickens and Carlyle*, University of Georgia Press, Athens, 1972.

GREENE, GRAHAM: 'The Young Dickens', in *The Lost Childhood and Other Essays*, Eyre & Spottiswoode, London, 1951.

HARBAGE, ALFRED: *A Kind of Power: The Shakespeare–Dickens Analogy*, Memoirs of the American Philosophical Society, Philadelphia, 1975.

HARDY, BARBARA: *The Moral Art of Charles Dickens*, Athlone Press, London, 1970.

HILL, NANCY K.: *A Reformer's Art: Dickens's Picturesque and Grotesque Imagery*, Ohio University Press, Athens and London, 1981.

HOLLINGTON, MICHAEL: *Dickens and the Grotesque*, Croom Helm, London, and Barnes & Noble, New York, 1984.

HORTON, SUSAN R.: *The Reader in the Dickens World*, Macmillan, London, 1980.

JEFFARES, A.N. (ED.): Special Dickens issue (guest editor John Butt) of *A Review of English Literature*, 2 (July 1961), Longman, London.

JOHNSON, EDGAR: *Charles Dickens, His Tragedy and Triumph*, 2 vols, Simon & Schuster, New York, 1952, Gollancz, London, 1953.

KAPLAN, FRED: *Dickens and Mesmerism: The Hidden Springs of Fiction*, Princeton University Press, Princeton, 1975.

KETTLE, ARNOLD: 'Oliver Twist', in *An Introduction to the English Novel*, vol. I, Hutchinson, London, 1951.

KINCAID, JAMES R.: *Dickens and the Rhetoric of Laughter*, Clarendon Press, Oxford, 1971.

LAMBERT, MARK: *Dickens and the Suspended Quotation*, Yale University Press, New Haven, 1981.

LEAVIS, F.R. and LEAVIS, Q.D.: *Dickens the Novelist*, Chatto & Windus, London, 1970.

LINDSAY, JACK: *Charles Dickens: A Biographical and Critical Study*, Dakers, London, 1950.

LUCAS, JOHN: *The Melancholy Man: A Study of Dickens's Novels*, Methuen, London, 1970.

MANNING, SYLVIA: *Dickens as Satirist*, Yale University Press, New Haven, 1971.

MILLER, J. HILLIS: *Charles Dickens: The World of His Novels*, Harvard University Press, Cambridge, Mass., 1957.

NEWMAN, S.J.: *Dickens at Play*, Macmillan, London, 1981.

NEWSOM, ROBERT: *Dickens on the Romantic Side of Familiar Things: Bleak House and the Novel Tradition*, Columbia University Press, New York, 1977.

NISBET, ADA B.: *Dickens and Ellen Ternan*, University of Calfornia Press, Berkeley and Los Angeles, 1952.

—— and NEVIUS, BLAKE (EDS): *Dickens Centennial Essays*, University of California Press, Berkeley and Los Angeles, 1971; special issue of *Nineteenth-Century Fiction*, 24 (March 1970).

ODDIE, WILLIAM: *Dickens and Carlyle: The Question of Influence*, Centenary Press, London, 1972.

ORWELL, GEORGE: 'Charles Dickens', in *Inside the Whale*, Gollancz, London, 1940, reprinted in various collections of his essays.

PAGE, NORMAN: *A Dickens Companion*, Macmillan, London, 1984.

PARTLOW JR., ROBERT B. (ED.): *Dickens the Craftsman: Strategies of Presentation*, Southern Illinois University Press, Carbondale, 1970.

PATTEN, ROBERT: *Charles Dickens and His Publishers*, Clarendon Press, Oxford, 1978.

PEARCE, ROY HARVEY (ED.): *Experience in the Novel*, includes lectures by Northrop Frye, K.J. Fielding, and J. Hillis Miller.

POPE, NORRIS: *Dickens and Charity*, Macmillan, London, 1978.

SANDERS, ANDREW: *Charles Dickens Resurrectionist*, Macmillan, London, 1982.

SHAW, G.B.: Introduction to *Hard Times*, Waverley edn, Waverley Book Co, London, 1912; also Introduction to *Great Expectations*, R. & R. Clark, Edinburgh, 1937, and other edns.

SLATER, MICHAEL: *Dickens and Women*, J.M. Dent, London, 1983.

—— (ED.) : *Dickens 1970*, Chapman & Hall, 1970.

SMITH, GRAHAME: *Dickens Money and Society*, University of California Press, Berkeley and Los Angeles, 1968.

STEIG, MICHAEL: *Dickens and Phiz*, Indiana University Press, Bloomington and London, 1978.

STEWART, GARRETT: *Dickens and the Trials of the Imagination*, Harvard University Press, Cambridge, Mass., 1974.

STONE, HARRY: *Dickens and the Invisible World: Fairy Tales, Fantasy and Novel-Making*, Indiana University Press, Bloomington and London, 1979.

SUCKSMITH, HARVEY P.: *The Narrative Art of Charles Dickens: The Rhetoric of Sympathy and Irony in His Novels*, Clarendon Press, Oxford, 1970.

SWINBURNE, A.C.: *Charles Dickens*, Chatto & Windus, London, 1913.

TILLOTSON, KATHLEEN: *'Dombey and Son'*, in *Novels of the Eighteen-Forties*, Clarendon Press, Oxford, 1954.

TOMLIN, E.W.F. (ED.): *Charles Dickens 1812-1870: A Centenary Volume*, Weidenfeld & Nicolson, 1969.

TRILLING, LIONEL: 'Little Dorrit', in *The Opposing Self*, Secker & Warburg, London, Viking Press, New York, 1955.

VOGEL, JANE: *Allegory in Dickens*, University of Alabama Press, University, 1977.

WALDER, DENNIS: *Dickens and Religion*, Allen & Unwin, 1981.

WELSH, ALEXANDER: *The City of Dickens*, Clarendon Press, Oxford, 1970.

WILSON, EDMUND: 'Dickens: The Two Scrooges', *New Republic*, 102 (March 1940), rev. and enlarged in *The Wound and the Bow*, Houghton Mifflin, Boston, 1941.

WORTH, GEORGE J.: *Dickensian Melodrama: A Reading of the Novels*, University of Kansas, Lawrence, 1978.

These lists are selective, but include works mentioned in the text. For recent work see Philip Collins's chapter in *Victorian Fiction, A Second Guide to Research*, ed. G.H. Ford (Modern Language Association, New York, 1978), Alan M. Cohn and K.K. Collins, *The Cumulative Dickens Checklist 1970-1979*, Whitson Publishing Co, Troy, N.Y., 1982, and current bibliographies such as those given annually by *Victorian Studies*, and the *Cumulative Bibliography of Victorian Studies*, Edmonton, Alberta, (1976 –), ed. B. Chaudhuri. Useful bibliographies for each novel will be found in the series of annotated *Unwin Dickens Companions*, general eds. Susan Chatto and Michael Cotsell (Allen & Unwin, London, 1986 –; beginning with *Bleak House, Edwin Drood* and *Our Mutual Friend*).

Periodicals

Valuable information, criticism and reviews of recent publications can be found in the *Dickensian*, now published thrice yearly (London, 1905 –; indexed by F.T. Dunn, 1976), *Dickens Studies Annual* (Carbondale, Ill., 1970 –; New York, 1980 –), and the *Dickens Quarterly* (Kentucky, 1984), formerly the *Dickens Studies Newsletter* (Carbondale, 1970 –).

Index

Further titles

A DICTIONARY OF LITERARY TERMS
MARTIN GRAY

Over one thousand literary terms are dealt with in this Handbook, with definitions, explanations and examples. Entries range from general topics (comedy, epic, metre, romanticism) to more specific terms (acrostic, enjambment, malapropism, onomatopoeia) and specialist technical language (catalexis, deconstruction, *haiku*, paeon). In other words, this single, concise volume should meet the needs of anyone searching for clarification of terms found in the study of literature.

Martin Gray is Lecturer in English at the University of Stirling.

AN INTRODUCTION TO LITERARY CRITICISM
RICHARD DUTTON

This is an introduction to a subject that has received increasing emphasis in the study of literature in recent years. As a means of identifying the underlying principles of the subject, the author examines the way in which successive eras and individual critics have applied different yardsticks by which to judge literary output. In this way the complexities of modern criticism are set in the perspective of its antecedents, and seen as only the most recent links in a chain of changing outlooks and methods of approach. The threads of this analysis are drawn together in the concluding chapter, which offers a blueprint for the practice of criticism.

Richard Dutton is Lecturer in English Literature at the University of Lancaster.

ENGLISH LITERATURE FROM THE THIRD WORLD
TREVOR JAMES

One of the most distinctive phenomena of English literature in this century is its expansion and diversification through the growth of numerous national literatures which, despite different historical contexts, are marked by their choice of English as the medium of expression. These literatures are dynamic witness to the cultural, social and political changes of this century, and in reacting to a variety of particular circumstances the writers offer fresh perspectives on experiences of universal interest. This Handbook provides a succinct guide to these new literatures, affording the reader an appreciation of the general shape – and the immensity – of the subject.

Trevor James is Senior Lecturer in English at the Darwin Institute of Technology, Australia.

THE ENGLISH NOVEL
IAN MILLIGAN

This Handbook deals with the English novel from the historical, thematic and technical points of view, and discusses the various purposes of authors and the manner in which they achieve their effects, as well as the role of the reader. The aim is to bring to light the variety of options at the novelist's disposal and to enhance the reader's critical and interpretive skills – and pleasure.

Ian Milligan is Lecturer in English at the University of Stirling.

PREPARING FOR EXAMINATIONS IN ENGLISH LITERATURE
NEIL McEWAN

This Handbook is specifically designed for all students of English literature who are approaching those final months of revision before an examination. The purpose of the volume is to provide a sound background to the study of set books and topics, placing them within the context and perspective of their particular genres. The author also draws on his wide experience as a teacher of English both in England and abroad to give advice on approaches to study, essay writing, and examination techniques.

Neil McEwan is Lecturer in English at the University of Qatar.

AN A·B·C OF SHAKESPEARE
His Plays, Theatre, Life and Times
P.C. BAYLEY

This is a systematic reference book to the background of Shakespeare. The aim has been to provide in one book an account of all the subjects and personalities which the student or theatre-goer is liable to encounter in the study of Shakespeare's plays and theatre. Fools, folios, theatres and music; mystery cycles and historical sources; summaries of all the plays; and details of Shakespeare's life and times – all these are presented in alphabetical order to provide easy reference, but in a form that will also reward the browser.

P. C. Bayley is Berry Professor of English at the University of St Andrews.

STUDYING CHAUCER
ELISABETH BREWER

The study of set books is always more interesting, rewarding and successful when the student is able to 'read around' the subject. But students faced with such a task will know the difficulties confronting them as they try to tackle work outside the prescribed texts. This Handbook is designed to help students to overcome this problem by offering guidance to the whole of Chaucer's output. An introduction to Chaucer's life and times is followed by a brief description and analysis of all his works, identifying the major issues and themes. The author also discusses contemporary literary conventions, and Chaucer's use of language.

Elisabeth Brewer is Lecturer in English at Homerton College of Education, Cambridge.

STUDYING SHAKESPEARE
MARTIN STEPHEN AND PHILIP FRANKS

Similar in aims to *Studying Chaucer*, this Handbook presents an account of Shakespeare's life and work in general, followed by a brief analysis of each of the plays by Shakespeare which might usefully be studied as background reading for a set book. Philip Franks then throws a different light on the study of Shakespeare by giving an account of his experiences of Shakespeare in performance from his perspective as a professional actor and member of the Royal Shakespeare Company.

Martin Stephen is Second Master at Sedbergh School; Philip Franks is a professional actor.

STUDYING MILTON
GEOFFREY M. RIDDEN

Studying Milton will appeal to the general reader and the student alike. Conscious of the growing interest in the literature and history of this period, and of the inaccuracy of the impressions that many people hold of it, the author has aimed to present a thorough background, encompassing historical circumstances as well as contemporary religious, political and literary thinking. Against this is set a survey and analysis of Milton's prose and poetry, including some of his lesser-known works, followed by a discussion of the changing views of Milton's output by successive generations of critics.

Geoffrey M. Ridden is Principal Lecturer in English at King Alfred's College, Winchester.

STUDYING THOMAS HARDY
LANCE ST JOHN BUTLER

This will be a valuable source for any student who wishes to survey the works of Thomas Hardy and draw together the threads of his substantial output. Hardy was a secretive man and he leaves a rather hazy image of himself compared to the vivid pictures of people, places and events evoked by much of his work – especially the Wessex novels. None the less, the circumstances of Hardy's life and the features of his art inform each other in a manner that is intriguing and rewarding to his readers, and the recurring themes of his novels, short stories and poems emerge with added significance. This Handbook provides access to the whole of Hardy's work and examines his stylistic devices, his use of landscape and dialect, his interest in the influence of change in people's lives – and his overall outlook on the world.

Lance St John Butler is Lecturer in English Studies at the University of Stirling.

The author of this Handbook

Kenneth J. Fielding is a graduate and D.Phil. of Oxford. He began teaching in colleges of education, and was appointed Saintsbury Professor of English Literature at the University of Edinburgh in 1966 and retired in 1984. He has been assistant editor and joint editor of volumes 1 and 5 of the Pilgrim edition of Dickens's *Letters* (1965–), edited Dickens's *Speeches* (1960; new edition 1988), and has written much about him, including *Charles Dickens, A Critical Introduction* (1965). He is also joint editor of the Duke–Edinburgh edition of *The Letters of Thomas and Jane Welsh Carlyle*, 18 volumes and on-going (1970–), of *Carlyle Past and Present* (1976), and of Carlyle's *The French Revolution* (1989).